A STORY

JILL MACDONALD grew up on a farm in Devonshire, UK. She trained as a singer, but later took to teaching English literature and poetry both in England and in India. She worked as an educational research officer at Exeter University, and published several articles and reports in collaboration with professors Pring and Wragg. More recently, HarperCollins published *A Battler All My Life*, which Jill transcribed and compiled from interviews with its co-author Joyce McCartan. Jill lives in Devonshire still, close to family roots.

A STORY FOR MUKTI

Based on the Letters of
His Grandfather Habib Tanvir

Introduction by Anna Tanvir
Foreword by Mukti

JILL MACDONALD

HarperCollins *Publishers* India

First published in India in 2016 by
HarperCollins *Publishers* India

Copyright © Jill MacDonald 2016

P-ISBN: 97-893-5264-070-6
E-ISBN: 97-893-5264-071-3

2 4 6 8 10 9 7 5 3 1

Jill MacDonald asserts the moral right to be
identified as the author of this work.

The views and opinions expressed in this book are the author's own
and the facts are as reported by her, and the publishers are not
in any way liable for the same.

All rights reserved. No part of this publication may be reproduced,
stored in a retrieval system, or transmitted, in any form or by any means,
electronic, mechanical, photocopying, recording or otherwise,
without the prior permission of the publishers.

HarperCollins *Publishers*
A-75, Sector 57, Noida, Uttar Pradesh 201301, India
1 London Bridge Street, London, SE1 9GF, United Kingdom
Hazelton Lanes, 55 Avenue Road, Suite 2900, Toronto, Ontario M5R 3L2
and 1995 Markham Road, Scarborough, Ontario M1B 5M8, Canada
25 Ryde Road, Pymble, Sydney, NSW 2073, Australia
195 Broadway, New York, NY 10007, USA

Typeset in 11.5/14.5 Garamond Premier Pro at
Manipal Digital Systems, Manipal

Printed and bound at
Thomson Press (India) Ltd

*To my three grandsons – Mukti, Kimani and Willoughby
with my love*

'Sir, more than kisses, letters mingle souls;
for thus, friends absent speak.'
—John Donne (1572–1631)

A Note on the Letters

Habib Tanvir's letters to Jill MacDonald have been reproduced in the original, complete with the original punctuation, abbreviations, spellings, etc., with only a few basic elements cleaned up.

Introduction

ANNA TANVIR

I first read my father's letters to my mother a few months after he had died. I was sitting in an aeroplane on my way to India to attend a festival celebrating his life and work that was being held in Bhopal in October 2009. It was a confusing moment. I hadn't had time to absorb the finality of my father's absence as I hadn't been to the state funeral some months earlier, nor was I sure why I was undertaking such a journey at this particular time. I simply felt I had to go to where he had lived, meet the actors of Naya Theatre whom I knew well, and meet my Indian family; I needed to be in India, on my father's home ground, to properly accept that he was no longer physically there.

My mother had handed me the photocopies of his letters to her to read on the journey and, as I sat on the plane, I was taken back to more than fifty years before, to discover the young person my father was at that time. As a child, I had threatened to tidy up my mother's drawer that contained a little red case full of creased letters that lay amongst a motley collection of woollen tights. My intention was to throw away the flimsy papers with their scrawly handwriting and arrange her clothes all neatly. It never occurred to me that this carefully preserved correspondence might give me the opportunity to know my father better after his death than when he was alive. I was grateful to my mother for preserving them for so many decades and allowing me to read them at last.

Throughout my stay in Bhopal, as I read those letters over and over again, I felt as though my father was with me. They allowed me to see into his heart in a way I had never before been able to, and many queries I had were clarified by his own handwritten words. Although I had discussed the past many times with my mother, and I was lucky enough to have talked to my father too about this period of his life, the letters took me into their story in a completely different way. They are not an interpretation of the past, and don't have the self-consciousness that naturally seeps in when you explain yourself as a parent to a child. They were not written for the general public but are the thoughts and feelings of an Indian artist conveyed to someone he grew to love, and we can trace the evolution of this love and his search for his own cultural identity through them.

It dawned on me that here was a unique insight into his thinking during his many years of travel through Europe. Perhaps it could shed light on all sorts of dilemmas faced by many Indians, particularly Indian artists, caught between their own culture and that of the West. These letters, written as they were to the same young woman over a decade, not only convey my father's feelings about the direction of his life at the time and give a glimpse of the person he was, but also show what an important role she played for him.

A few years before my father died, my mother went to visit him in Bhopal. They sat in a restaurant with two very good friends of his who afterwards told me they were fascinated by the rapport between the two of them. They wondered if she had been a source of inspiration for him throughout his life. I think the answer lies in my father's own words in the many letters he wrote to her. It is clear that he's replying directly to one of her letters when his tone is inspired and eloquent, but when there is a gap in the communication because he has not heard from her for some time, his sense of isolation is palpable. My mother was by no means the only woman in his life, but evidently their relationship was deep and enduring for both of them.

The correspondence is one-sided as my mother's letters have not survived, but through his writing, we glimpse an enticingly sketchy portrait of her thoughts and feelings as her life unfolds. The answers my father's letters provided about himself led me to wonder about her. Would she fill in some of the missing pieces in the story these letters told? What was it like for her, a young artistic girl, to meet an Indian poet during the 1950s? What was she doing during these years? What sort of relationship could they have developed, divided by culture, geography and an age gap? How did her Australian cowboy father respond to her choice? What did my father and she talk about? How did they ever spend time together, given the prejudices of the era?

My own children, some of my father's closest friends and many other people, particularly Indian women, have shown great interest in looking for the answers to these questions. My sons are the only grandchildren my father had, and he grew very fond of them before he died, but they didn't have time to talk to him at length about his youth or about his meeting with their grandmother, and in any case they were in awe of him. It's very hard for children to imagine their grandparents as young people, in love, with all the difficulties and confusion that go with that state of mind. They would find it hard to imagine the practical difficulties of meeting up at the time, or the misunderstandings that would have come about through cultural differences and the prejudice my parents met with when walking along the pavement together in London. They would also struggle to understand the worries that my Western grandparents had about their daughter being involved in such an unusual relationship.

All our questions and curiosity meant that we came together, my sons and I, to encourage my mother to write her story. She was very reluctant to do so, as she couldn't see that the story of her youth, bound up as it was with my father, could be of any real interest to anyone. She found it painful and sometimes overwhelming re-reading a correspondence that she hadn't looked at for over half a century, and had little wish for her own story to be known. My eldest son Mukti has a close relationship with his grandmother, and eventually it was he who was able to persuade her that her story was worth telling.

She finally agreed to write it down in a very long letter to Mukti, knowing that by doing so, future generations would have an authentic record of their antecedents. For my mother, this was the only form she was comfortable with, so Mukti and she sat together and he talked to her about her past and asked many questions. He was only seventeen at the time, and my mother was very aware of the generation gap and the huge changes that have taken place in society since she was the same age as him. So she has tried to bridge this gap with explanations of how different things were for her at that time. By then Mukti had visited India several times, which gave him the opportunity to forge his own links, and he already had a feeling for his grandfather's culture and background.

When my father died, there was very little mention of my existence in the media or that of my children. This didn't seem to matter much except that there were a few newspaper articles that gave inaccurate statements about my mother. One journalist even went so far as to suggest that I was the daughter of a French actress who had a brief relationship with my father during the fifties. Members of my Indian family simply had no idea who my mother was or what happened between her and my father, and what she had meant to him. Whatever account I might give of what I understood of my own background was difficult for them to accept, since he had not talked with them openly about this part of his life. These letters may help clear the air about some of these misunderstandings.

Although this book is a love story, the letters also give a singular insight, as I've said, into the thoughts of a great artist and the struggle he faced with re-establishing himself in his own country. They allow us to know the man and not just the theatre director and poet. I am not sure any other form of writing could be so immediate and revealing. There's no doubt he had led a remarkable life. Many people have written about him, and his fame goes beyond Indian borders. But my mother's story, to my mind, is also remarkable, not just for her connection with my father, but as an example of an independent-minded young woman who paid no heed to the conventions of her day and followed her heart, resulting in my existence.

Foreword

Mukti

My first memory of my Indian grandfather, Habib, is of when he came to stay in my other grandparents' house in Gloucestershire. I must have been about three years old. That was in 1995. There's a photo of me meeting him for the first time in the garden, with Mama and Kim. Kim was very small, just a few months old, and you can see he's attached (page xix) to Mama's front in a sling with his legs hanging down. I hadn't a clue who Habib was, but I can see him still, in my mind's eye, sitting on the stairs smoking his pipe. The small room in the corner where he stayed smelled of pipe-smoke for ages after he left, and is still known as 'Habib's room'. I call it that too. For me, the whole pipe-smoking thing, which you don't see often these days, made him a mysterious, mystical figure.

Later, he did appear in our house in France from time to time. Mum and Gran talked about him, which gave me the idea he must be important, but I didn't know exactly where he fitted in. He didn't stay in my mind as a person, like the grandparents I was used to. He was more of a presence, a figure. Then, in 2007, we met him at Heathrow with Nageen, his daughter and Mum's half-sister, on the way to France for his last but one stay. And I thought to myself, 'He does have an amazing gravitas, doesn't he – maybe in his way of speaking.' He had an incredible voice. He came out of the plane and the first thing he talked about, having not seen me for eight years or so, was the fact that he'd had to spend nine or ten hours travelling without being able to smoke. He was in a wheelchair but looked stylish nevertheless, wearing his black beret like a Frenchman. I wheeled him into a little room set aside for smokers, and after a bit he came out looking a lot happier. While Nageen and Gran were trying to sort the luggage out, I pushed him in the wheelchair around the airport very fast, for fun. He enjoyed that.

He was very calm and spoke very slowly, which meant there was an importance about everything he said; it was a commanding manner. While he was staying with us in France, he gave a talk at the university in Tours about globalization. It was very vague, I must say, but he looked the part absolutely, and maintained the commanding presence. At that point, I couldn't tell how seriously he took himself: who was the real person and who was the persona? Perhaps when you become famous you don't know yourself. That is a thought that I will hang on to in my own life, just in case.

To tell the truth, I never felt I really knew Habib, but reading through those early letters has brought me a lot closer to him. I know I want to act and to travel everywhere. I don't want to be pinned down, and those characteristics could well have been inherited from him. It will be interesting to see how much my brothers have inherited. I have read somewhere that the influence of grandparents can be stronger than even that of parents. I'll just have to wait and see.

Habib meeting Mukti

1

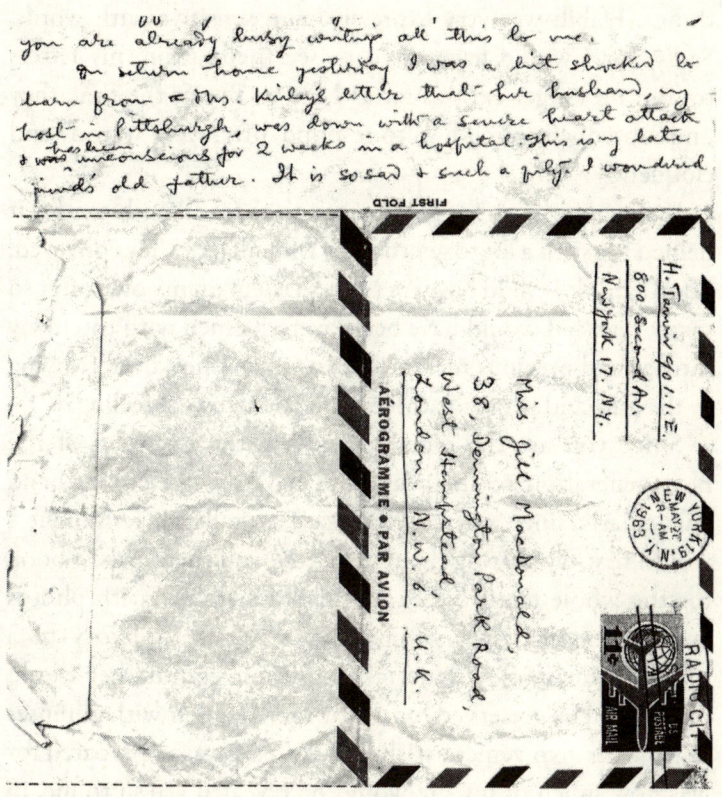

Dearest Mukti,

You tell me that letters are practically non-existent in your life. It's all texting and emails. What I'm about to write to you looks as though it will be a very long letter indeed. You'll need to take a deep breath...

In my youth, letters were all the rage, including love letters, of which there are many here. And being a poet, amongst other things, Habib was very expressive and sensitive with words. Sadly, for I would have loved to see them again, my letters to him no longer exist as far as I know. But at the time they undoubtedly inspired him to respond, often very warmly and eloquently.

I must thank you for going through them all with me, for it helped me such a lot to get to grips with all that they conveyed. I don't think I could have ever reread them on my own after so many years – I would have been overwhelmed with too many intense and precious memories. And then one can start living in the past and get stuck there, which is an awful feeling.

Since you are the oldest grandson, the guardian of the next generation so to speak, and have an open mind, and particularly since you are very easy to talk to, I thought I would first try sharing them with you, and then make a book for the whole family, as beautiful as possible – with photos and adding my own commentaries. Thus the story of a magnificent journey undertaken by your grandfather would unfold and be preserved for the future, together with glimpses of my own involvement with him. What I wasn't prepared for was how much of my life would be revealed afresh to me, in a way that would have been impossible without such intimate reminders. It has made my writing proceed rather haltingly, for one cannot hurry the reliving of some of the most important moments of one's life.

When I first unearthed Habib's letters, some two months after he died, I was too moved to have any thoughts at all as to what I might do with them. But of one thing I was sure: that

I should not keep them all to myself. They simply jumped to life – beautifully written, agonizingly so at times, lyrical and conversational. Stuffed into a small red writing case, battered and worn, they had travelled with me throughout my various moves for more than fifty years. Placed there haphazardly, some crumpled, some with stamps missing, the first one had arrived when I was just sixteen. There were more than fifty, the main body of which covered nine crucial years of our lives. The story they tell is two-fold: of our love affair that endured despite its fragile footing, and of Habib's very adventurous journey that forged his ideas about theatre, for which he was to become so well known.

As he himself recognized, his revolutionary thoughts regarding every aspect of Indian theatre would not have developed in the particular way they did had he not undertaken that journey. For over two years he rambled around Europe, moving from country to country, earning his living as best as he could, sometimes staying a while if there was good theatre to explore and a way of surviving financially, sometimes being forced to move on as a result of difficulties ranging from political upheaval to a dire lack of funds. His tenacity and the sheer excitement of travel kept him going.

There are so many different emotions, events and states of being expressed in these letters – loneliness and struggle, warm friendships and valuable meetings, huge practical discomforts and challenges, the sub-zero temperatures he encountered in Russia and Poland being not the least of them. But it was all worth it for the rewards in terms of life experience. The insights he gained into different forms of theatre influenced him ever after, allowing him space for his own thinking and the confidence to find his own voice, neither to copy nor to emulate, as he put it, but to combine and renew.

When I think of Habib at this time, he reminds me of Voltaire's hero Candide, who searched the world for a true reflection of himself and ended up successfully cultivating his own back garden. Habib's eventual return to India to gather up his very first actors from the region of his childhood and form Naya Theatre is, in a way, the same story.

So you see, it was a very significant time for him and I think his letters convey this in the most exciting and authentic way possible. But, to go back to the beginning: you asked me how we met. I'll tell you about that...

I first met Habib in Edinburgh in 1955 and yes, he was awfully older than I was, twice my age in fact, at thirty-two. Did that matter? No, in fact he did not seem that much older because he was not in the least bit staid. He was slight and intense and full of a rather innocent sense of fun. That first meeting – it was, needless to say, a most important encounter that I remember vividly – came about because my sister was up in Edinburgh at the time of the Festival. She wrote to me inviting me to stay with her, mentioning that there was a handsome and most engaging Indian lodging in the same house who, she was sure, I'd like to meet. The only difficulty, she added, was that he tended to get up very late and come back very late at night, so was easily missed. After twice missing him due to getting up too early, the third morning I forced myself to stay in bed until after 10 o'clock.

On entering the dining room there he was, with a wide, welcoming smile, a deliciously gravelly voice like no other, and elegantly clothed in a loose khadi shirt of deepest red.

Who could not help but be drawn to all of that, especially in the case of a young girl already fascinated by his country? And the rapport was instant, keeping us talking until lunchtime. So that was the beginning of a very long romance which affected many lives and created a new one – but all that is for later.

It was about a year after that first meeting that Habib left England to begin his epic tour of Europe, for what he thought would be a spell of a few months. He wasn't to return for over two years, but before he set off we had seen quite a bit more of each other and started up a heartfelt correspondence.

Your observation that such a romance could not exist these days, in the same way, was interesting and also startling. For nowadays, if there are so few letters passing between people, how can there be a record of what they really felt? How can biographies be written as richly as they have been without recourse to letters? Think of the many wonderfully evocative letters composed by ordinary soldiers during wartime to families who feared they might never see them again, and how treasured these letters were and continue to be in many of those families.

Throughout history, letters have been a major source of information, often of the most intimate kind. They have always been around, but now you say they are rare, and I believe you. But I must admit I am glad to have been born at a time when they weren't. To this day, the sight of an unopened letter addressed to me, with strange, exotic stamps, makes my heart jump. Habib's were particularly enticing – not only for what they said but also for how they looked, coming from all parts of Europe and always handwritten.

As well as providing insights into our correspondence, I would like to tell you something about the times we were living through – so different from the era in which you have grown up. Because my letters to Habib no longer exist, I can only write my part of the story as vividly as my memory will allow.

As far as I know, Habib never finished his own memoirs. He spoke about an autobiography and tried to get on with it for many years. Unfortunately, there were too many interruptions in his life to allow for the sustained spell of quiet he needed in order to complete the second and third volumes. His very last, shakily handwritten message to your mother expressed both a wish and a firm intention to get them done in the stillness of the French countryside. But this was not to be. He died a few months after she received this letter, having become too ill to travel. It's very good to know, and I think you'll agree, that the warm and insightful outpourings contained in his letters have not suffered the same uncertain fate.

Habib in his twenties and Jill aged sixteen

46, Princess Victoria Street, Clifton, Bristol, 8
6th October 55

My dear Jill
At last I have been able to collect myself enough to write to you. I am more or less settled in Bristol and started working steadily. I have got a lovely room and I have done it up quite well. You must see it. That's an invitation now. When are you coming? I promise a wonderful cup of real 'Indian' tea, if you would care for it.

Oh yes, I enjoyed staying with the Century Theatre – peeling potatoes and washing dishes in the kitchen and talking and living with players and watching plays. On my way back I stopped at Birmingham and saw yet one more play – that of the famous Repertory Theatre there. In 2 days in London still two more plays.

In the last 2 weeks in Bristol however, I saw only one. But there is nothing much to see here. There is a lot of work in the school to do though, and very interesting work too like mask-making, jewellery-making, costume-making, modelling, technical drawing – oh, ever so many things.

But life is not all work. That is the snag. The evenings are dull. There are no friends as yet. The process of making friends is slow, isn't it? Must take time. At the present, I am spending most of my evenings in the library.

But I like Bristol. It is nice and quiet for a change. When you miss friends, you go and see a film.

But tell me something about yourself. Have you started work in right earnest? And do you like it? Do let me know all about it – what you have to do, how many times you have to go to London and so forth.

> *I wonder if you would be in London on the 5th, 6th, and 7th November. I am planning to come during the holidays then and would love to see you if you are there.*
>
> With love
>
> Yours sincerely
> Habib

I was thrilled to get this first letter and no doubt answered it immediately and copiously, for I very much enjoyed writing letters. Habib had already explained to me that he had just left RADA, the Royal Academy of Dramatic Art, with the firm belief that what he was learning there would not be of any use to him once he got back to India. With a successful production of *Agra Bazaar* already behind him, he felt a cultural gap of understanding between his increasingly radical approach to theatre and the very English and traditional training he was offered in London.

The Bristol Old Vic obviously suited him a lot better, with its practical, hands-on approach and the chance to work on a variety of projects. He loved getting together with other people creatively and doing very ordinary things as well. It was the sort of atmosphere he always enjoyed and I understood easily why, later in his life, he chose to live amongst his own troupe of tribal actors, cheek by jowl, even though it was a most unusual thing to do at the time.

Mukti, you will probably think I was very foolish for missing such an opportunity, but I did not visit that cosy-sounding room, or at that point share the cup of real Indian tea. I couldn't, much as I wanted to. Encouraged by my parents, I had rather inanely got myself enrolled into a course for a whole year to study, of all things, 'house-wifery', at what was then called a 'finishing school' in Surrey. You will have never heard of such a school, I feel sure, so I'll explain its aims, which will seem very old-fashioned to someone like you. The idea was to train middle- to upper-class girls in the arts of cooking, sewing, dusting and walking gracefully in preparation for the 'good' marriage that might, with luck, await them. I don't think it could be called a success in my case, for the 'good' marriage – to someone well off and presentable – somehow eluded me, while the course itself nearly did finish me off by being so dreadfully narrow and boring. I greatly envied Habib his so much more stimulating occupations. So what on earth was I doing there? Passing the time until I was old enough, at seventeen, to go on to Dartington Hall to train as a singer.

Even so, there were some positive aspects. The location of my finishing school did offer a few opportunities for escape, which were essential for survival. Being surrounded by a high wall and containing more than a hundred girls and an all-women staff, it seemed a million miles from the 'big city'. But it was actually only half an hour away by train, and that is where Habib managed to get to now and again, travelling from Bristol, to see theatre.

Some of the girls, of an evening, would be driven to standing on tiptoe and peeping over the wall in the hopes of making eye contact with some young male, who might even return to make the same eye contact another evening. As it happened, some were even more daring, climbing over the wall in the dead of night to further their acquaintanceship that had begun so like that of Pyramus and Thisbe, peering through holes in the wall at each other.

My own escapes were truly spectacular, I thought. Several times in the course of that year, I went up to London to meet Habib and watch live plays of which I had little experience, having been brought up in the middle of the countryside on a farm in Devon, miles away from anywhere. Joan Littlewood's *Oh What a Lovely War* was on then, in 1955. The memory of it is very clear, not only because it was such a noisy, rough and lively production, but also because I was so keyed up for it. Knowing that Habib was the 'expert' on theatre, I thought I'd better pay every bit of attention and be ready with a few bright and hopefully discerning comments at the end. So, being on the edge of my seat was a very real state of affairs. However, when the moment came, he was peacefully slumbering at my side as he had done for most of the performance, only stirring himself when the clapping started, to ask what had happened. He had been up too late the evening before, he explained. This was something of a relief to me.

Subsequently, I gained a lot more confidence in offering my thoughts on a variety of plays that we saw together. I soon learned that Habib was not interested in impressing anyone with his great knowledge, so I need not fear appearing too ignorant. Anyone could make a simple comment and so long as it was genuine and not pretentious, he would listen and, as often as not, nod gravely.

I remember well the very first play I saw with Habib, because it was an odd occasion. It was *Macbeth* at Stratford and I only saw half of it. I had turned up unexpectedly at the theatre because it was a last-minute decision to go. We had known each other for only a week in Edinburgh and I was a shy person, so I could not make up my mind to accept the invitation. But then I did and luckily came across Habib in the crowded auditorium. He had only one ticket and no more were available, so we shared it – he went in for the first half and I for the second. He very much wanted to see how the witches managed themselves on stage, but for myself, not having an especially soft spot for witches, I didn't mind missing that scene. So that is how we arranged it.

You are right, Mukti, there is an air of loneliness coming through in this letter. I think your grandfather's sense of isolation must have arisen partly as a result of his circumstances. He had arrived at RADA with high hopes that it would give him the instruction he needed, only to find this was not the case.

That first year must have been a struggle. Bristol, where he was at the time of this letter, was much better, but he hasn't been there long enough to make real friends. He's right – the process does take time. Perhaps being the creative person that he was had something to do with it as well. As an innovator in the broadest sense, he must have found it difficult to find like-minded people, and perhaps that would have made him feel like an outsider. As it happened, this sensation dogged him in its severest form when he was to return to India, and he describes it graphically in later letters.

46, Princess Victoria Street,
Clifton, Bristol, 8
4th December 55

My dear Jill,
Thanks for your lovely letter, which I took more than 6 weeks to reply to. I am sorry. I was awfully busy.

I shall be in Dublin on the 18th. For a week or so. I wrote to Carley to get digs booked for me. She writes that your whole family will be there at that time. Does that mean you will be there too. Oh, how wonderful! Do let me know if this is not too good to be believed.

I am busy making masks and producing a play. Do you want a mask for yourself so sometimes when you don't want to be recognized and want to frighten people, you can wear it?

I am glad you are learning all the little artistries of house-keeping under a very hard discipline. Do you good, don't you think?

No, Bristol is as dull as ever and promises to remain so – no friends, no prospects as yet. There were 2 fellows in the house here, nice chaps, but they too are shifting next week. Oh well!!!

I am not going to grow a beard and all that but I am certainly expecting you to grow into an accomplished housewife soon, looking like simply growing all over with an immense knowledge of all the little intricacies of the great art.

Wish you all luck and Godspeed too.

I am glad you like your music lessons. I am sure they are interesting.

Envy you!

With all my love,
Yours Habib

Carley

Your great-aunt Carley knew Habib before I did. She was, and still is, tall and beautiful. He remained fond of her always and teased me by saying that if she had not been so tall he would have pursued her instead of me. He particularly liked the way she scoffed, which she certainly did – and still does – with aplomb. If scoffing were an art, he considered that Carley had mastered it excellently well.

The term 'housewife' sounds so dreadfully dull, I am not surprised that as a young person you find it difficult to stomach. But in the 1950s it was not so unusual to take the art of running a household quite seriously. There were many such establishments similar to my school, running successful courses for middle-class young ladies. But I fear – and you were right to point it out, Mukti – that with its heavy emphasis on cleaning and ironing, mine was probably not one of the smartest. I don't think the pupils who enrolled there were expecting to land up married with lots of servants. Certainly, *I* wasn't.

In any case, the coming of the Second World War had put a stop to that sort of existence for most families. Having experienced alternative employment of a useful nature in the outside world, many working women had no great wish to return to 'service', and who could blame them. To have a cook or a maid in the '50s had become something of a luxury. All the same, you were expected to learn ways of doing things properly in the house and if your mother had not passed on any of her skills (or maybe she had none), then a finishing school was a possible answer. At least then you could direct the servants, if you were rich enough to employ some; otherwise, the hope was that you would be equipped to cope without.

Rather surprisingly, the old-fashioned traditions of being presented to the Queen and of 'coming out' were still practised. Debutantes, as they were called, enjoyed a season of dances, dinners and outings, hopefully in London, where they could mix with other young people of wealthy background. And of course, there was always the possibility of being introduced to a suitable husband. Now my mother, known as Bar, 'came out' and, being exceptionally shy and serious by nature, loathed every moment of it. Just in case you're getting in a muddle, she was your great-grandmother, born in 1912, just before the First World War. There is a wonderful picture of her in her 'presentation' dress for meeting the Queen; it was Queen Mary at the time. She looks fantastic, but if the truth be told, she probably felt quite sick, because she always felt sick, even as a child, when she had to take part in social events.

Her mother, Granny (your great-great-grandmother), put it down to Bar being a redhead. People with red hair had a few genes missing, she declared, which made them a lot more sensitive than ordinary people. I'm not sure how far this is true but she certainly did have that extra sensitivity.

My mother in her 'Coming Out' robe

To get back to Habib's letter, I have a feeling his comments concerning my efforts to master the domestic arts stemmed from kindness. He was making the best of it for my sake, knowing that I was actually bored stiff. Later, I started training as a singer and in this he was genuinely interested.

The trip to Dublin that he mentions never came off. Plans were always changing and this time it was Habib who didn't make it. I should have loved him to meet my Irish family. To this day they are wonderfully entertaining. My aunt Chris was a very good raconteur. She had not yet written her bestselling autobiography, *The Past Is Myself*, a moving, vivid description of her experiences as an 'enemy alien' living with her family all through the war years in Berlin. We were a close family, having lodged together as seven cousins and two lots of parents in our grandmother's house after 1945, and the closeness never disappeared after those years. I thought Habib would have so enjoyed a stay on my aunt and uncle's farm in Ireland, which Carley could have arranged. He would certainly have appreciated my family being great storytellers, as he was himself.

169, Fordwych Road, N.W.2
30.4.56

My dear Jill,
I was overwhelmed by your very, very, very sweet letter. Thanks.

I am doing a course here in London and I am sorry I can't come. It is so very disappointing for me – I had planned to come – but this unexpected change from Bristol to London cost me my Easter Holidays. What a shame!

If I have time, then I might visit Dublin in July, but no one would be there then, would you?

Shall be in London up to the 15th of June, when I finish my course. I may spend a few more weeks here in England after that, if I have money left, and then go to France, Germany, Switzerland and so on, for a few months – on my way to India. I may sail by November or December. Of course I shall come to London for taking my boat.

Now tell me when do you come to London next, or don't you. I must see you before I leave this country. That is absolutely essential. But can't I? You must have grown up quite a bit in the last one year you know. I am dying to see you.

My behaviour has been quite beastly I admit Jill – I apologize for not writing to you this long – and please accept my belated but heart-felt thanks for your really exquisite Christmas card and letter. Hope you got mine.

It is a very exciting theatre season here in London this year and my course is very interesting too. So I am alright really.

I can never thank you too much for your affectionate letter which I needed I suppose.

With love,

Yours
Habib

You will write again, won't you Jill?

I was an enthusiastic letter writer and Habib's efforts were definitely spasmodic. I think he often found it difficult to keep up, being tremendously busy and on the move, as he nearly always was, about which he was keenly aware and unhappy. Over time, each of us was always a little bit frightened that the other one would give up – or had given up. If I had no news of him I would worry that something had happened to him or he'd found another girlfriend; if he didn't hear from me, he thought that was because I was fed up with such long silences. At one point, I threatened not to write to him unless I had received his news, but he was so upset with this arrangement that I had to relent. In any case, I enjoyed writing too much to stick to my word! Months passed before I would hear from him, which was practically a lifetime as far as I was concerned.

Sadly, we never did manage to visit Ireland together and I'm not sure if Habib ever got there at all.

169, Fordwych Road, N.W.1
21.5.56

Hello Jill!
How are your measles now? It's a shame I did not catch any.
Are you working as hard as I am? When do you take rest from it all and spend a week-end in London? You must do that and let me know well in advance. I shall look forward to it. Would you like me to arrange accommodation?
I have been seeing many plays – some very good ones. I feel desperate about plays here, for soon I am to say goodbye to your country, perhaps for ever.
Well, I am writing this in a great hurry. Do let me hear from you soon.

All the best and much love.

Yours
Habib

I couldn't get myself up to London because of the measles, which were undoubtedly of the German sort because I'd had the other kind in childhood. As soon as I was better I would make the effort, I thought. But he'd mentioned that he would be going away 'perhaps for ever', which alarmed me.

Was there something going on then between us, you ask? Yes, of course there was. Lots! What else would you expect? As young people, we were not as restrained then as you might imagine. You just didn't tell your parents what was happening in your life in case they disapproved. If you were wise, you kept all talk of romance for your sympathetic friends, whose preoccupations were mostly just the same.

169, Fordwych Rd., N.W.2
11.6.56

My dear Jill,
Sorry for this delay. I have been busy with my exam, and the school show, just over today.
  But I have been thinking about you, Jill. Yes, and missing you.
  Do let me know what time you arrive in London and when you leave. I shouldn't come with you, I don't think – but some other time perhaps. Most probably I shan't be able to see you on Friday, but perhaps you could stay a day in London on your way back from Devon. I should love to see you before leaving for Europe. Do let me know when you get back and if it would be possible for you to stay. You see I don't know how many months I shall be in Europe. Possibly up to December – and then I sail. The dream of going to Devon or to Edinburgh seems impossible.
  Do you know when Carley comes to Devon?
  And how are you, my dear Jill? Have you been good? I bet you have.
  What else?
  Don't forget to reply.
  I am sending a p.o. For £1. Thanks so much for the loan.

  A lot of love, Yours Habib

Sanduck farm in Devonshire

Because I was proud of him and excited about having such an unusual boyfriend, I was hoping Habib would come down to Devon to meet my family. I was passing through London on the way home and had suggested he accompany me. Instinctively, I had felt there would be more to talk about to my parents and less to keep secret if he did. In any case, Devon was plainly a wonderful place to go. The farm was there, with all its space and greenery, and June was one of the best months, with the hedges full of flowers along either side of tiny, narrow country lanes, and everything growing. I thought he would never have seen such a setting, so different from the India I imagined.

Yes, you're right, I do remember being a bit anxious about such a meeting. Mum would be fine and welcoming. She was interested in Indian culture, having been a great fan of the philosopher and sage Jiddu Krishnamurti all her life, and I knew she would like Habib and not be prejudiced. My father was entirely different. He was an Australian, brought up in the outback on a cattle ranch, where he had been encouraged to adopt an attitude towards the Aboriginal workers that was shockingly racist. This was not unusual given his background, but it did not help that he was entirely uninterested in different cultures. If a person was coloured, they might as well be an Aborigine as far as he was concerned. He was reclusive and erratic, even more so after his stressful experiences as a pilot during the war. Given to abruptness if he didn't approve of a guest, he'd go so far as to march right out of the room on occasion. Even bringing English friends back home could be an uncomfortable experience. So you see, Mukti, my worries regarding bringing Habib to meet my family were well founded. All the same, I badly wanted to introduce him, despite the risks.

My father in flying gear during the war

(undated) 169, Fordwych Road,
N.W.2
(Tel: Gladstone 5035)

My dear Jill,
Delighted!

I don't care about your silly measles and don't mind what you would call 'going to bed with them'. I should love to see you this week and I have indeed made a supreme effort. Can you meet me at 2 P.M. On Saturday 12th. Just outside the Old Vic Theatre (which is near the Waterloo Station – Northern Line)? I have secured 2 seats for Othello – it is the last day for 'Othello'. The show begins at 2.30 P.M. So we can have coffee or something just before the show; and if you can be so good as to have heaps of time at your disposal, we shall spend a quiet evening somewhere and have dinner and so on.

In case you are doing nothing worthwhile in that wretched place except getting bored with yourself and should like to come earlier on, just give me a ring on Saturday morning about 10 a.m. Or any time you like – and I should be delighted. Then perhaps you might come along to Kilburn about 12 o'clock or so and I could meet you at the station.

I am busy but not for you. Looking forward a great deal to seeing you. Do you look different now? I hope not.

With love,

Yours
Habib

NB: This letter is undated and sadly I don't remember that these arrangements took place.

Addressed to my finishing school, this letter produced a flurry of interest and a commendable surge of envy amongst my friends. I showed it to those who were closest and they were gratifyingly impressed. To go out with an Indian who was undoubtedly handsome and so much older was exotic enough, but that he could plan a day so well, buy tickets for the theatre in advance, make what he called 'a supreme effort' and write heart-warming utterances such as 'I am busy, but not for you' – those were really things to be proud of.

Many questions followed. Was I in love with him? Was he with me? What did my parents have to say about it? What was it like going out with an Indian? I didn't at that point know exactly how to respond to all their urgent inquiries, except for the first, to which the answer was definitely 'yes'. As for going out with an Indian, this seemed to me a wonderfully adventurous thing to be doing and I longed to know how my love affair would develop. But I was anxious, for during many of our meetings I had the feeling there was something almost sprite-like about Habib, that he might just disappear into the blue, not to be seen again, and I tried to warn myself not to give my heart away too quickly in case this was so. As you will see, Mukti, my uncertainties were not baseless, for it seems he shared a similar feeling about himself and hints at this several times in letters to come.

*169, Fordwych Rd.,
N.W.2
20.6.56.*

*My dear Jill,
    I was delighted to get your letter. A lovely letter too! Thanks.
    I am prepared to make a supreme effort but that can only be after 10 P.M. On Saturday as my examination*

continues till then. I should love to meet you then if you like but I do wish you had to go nowhere at all. Look! Are you staying in the same place? And how long do you stay? Would you be here on Sunday all the time as well? During most of the day on Sunday I have my exam again, but later perhaps I could be free. Then on Monday I fly to France. And then perhaps Germany. I may be away a month or a couple of months or six months – I don't know. So in any case, meet you this time anyhow I must. Now you help me and tell me how best I can do it. Would you like me to make arrangements for your stay or would you let me know how to contact you when you get here. And what time do you get here? Please answer all my questions. I am most anxious to see you again and talk to you. (I got a 'Starred Certificate of all-round excellence' for my work on the course in London). All the best and lots and lots of love,

Yours Habib

At the time I probably did not understand how complicated my feelings were, all mixed up with fear and huge anticipation, but I remember our last meeting in London before Habib took off for Europe being difficult because of them – intense and very precious moments, laced through with bleakness and distress. Here was someone so important, indeed crucial to my life, hardly grasped and already slipping away. All our arrangements seemed to go wrong too, with no cosy restaurant waiting to receive us where we could have relaxed and talked properly; cinema not showing what we thought; weather suddenly more like winter than June.

I stayed the night in my uncle's house, a smart and rather brittle place in Hampstead, and felt very uncomfortable and lonely there. I guess I simply didn't dare accept Habib's invitation to lodge with him, well knowing what the outcome would be, and that the next morning he'd be gone out of my reach, perhaps 'for ever'.

As you can imagine, I felt terrible travelling by train alone on Sunday early evening after that particular trip, back to my school, that 'wretched place'. How could one possibly take seriously what was on offer there, under such circumstances? It had not engaged me to start with, except for the cooking which was always fine and meaningful. Now, the rest of it seemed downright silly. Thank goodness it would all be coming to an end soon. There was just one more month to go.

c/o The Grindlays Bank Ltd.,
54, Parliament Street, London S.W.1 26.6.56

My dear Jill
Sorry I could not get the time to get a p.o. But I am sure the cash is safe. Thanks.
   I am off. Be seeing you. I have started missing you already. Do look after yourself and drop me a line whenever you feel like. I shall be writing to you about my programme as soon as it is clear in my own mind.

Bye bye.

Lots of kisses,
Yours
Habib

This was brisk – to me it signalled a time to pull myself together, get on with practical living, make plans. My need for more independence was becoming very pressing. That is something you will well understand, Mukti, for I was seventeen, just the same age as you are now. Not that I felt very capable of independent living, equipped with a deep aversion to dusting and only a few cookery skills. But I believed, and still do even in these tough times, that you can get a job if you show enough enthusiasm and confidence, and that to be truly independent, the only solution is to start by earning one's own money.

2

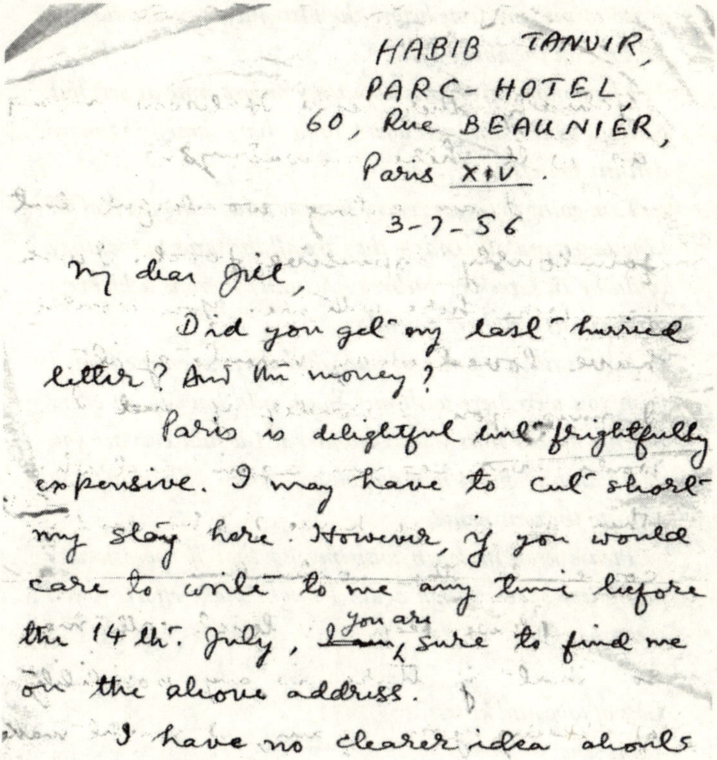

[handwritten letter:]

HABIB TANVIR,
PARC-HOTEL,
60, Rue BEAUNIÉR,
Paris XIV.

3-7-56

My dear Jill,
  Did you get my last hurried letter? And the money?
  Paris is delightful and frightfully expensive. I may have to cut short my stay here. However, if you would care to write to me any time before the 14th. July, ~~I am~~ you are sure to find me on the above address.
  I have no clearer idea about

PARC-HOTEL
60, Rue Beaunier,
Paris XIV
3.7.56

My dear Jill
Did you get my last hurried letter? And the money?

Paris is delightful but frightfully expensive. I may have to cut short my stay here. However, if you would care to write to me any time before the 14th July, you are sure to find me on the above address.

I have no clearer idea about my programme as yet, but perhaps by the time you write, I may have something more definite to say.

I am going to theatre every evening and seeing plays of all languages and all lands – they are all the same to me; they could be in Greek or Hebrew. Actually there is a Hebrew company as well here nowadays.

I am eating wonderful but fabulously expensive food. I wish you were here with me. You would have loved every minute of it. I miss you. I wonder if I would ever see you again and when. When do you go home? Why don't you come to the continent?

Please keep in touch with me, so that if there is any possibility of seeing you again I might make efforts – yes, supreme efforts.

Lots of love and kisses,
Yours sinc'
HT

How was it that I didn't manage to get to Paris, which sounded like a paradise of joyful indulgence? There were several reasons. First, my awful school was not yet finished. I had housewifery tests (of great silliness), which could hardly be called exams, that were right at the end of term when I should have so loved to be on that journey.

An ironing test:

Q. In what order should a man's shirt be ironed?

A. From right side front to left side pushing it away from you, then the sleeves and finally, MOST important, the collar.

There were cooking tests which did make some sense, and then a dress show to demonstrate our deportment. I would have liked a dusting test just to see how it could be set up and if I could have passed it, but that was not on the curriculum.

Second, I knew nobody who just hopped off to Paris by themselves, wonderful though the idea sounded. Nowadays it would not be so strange a thing to do, just to meet up with someone you loved and have a happy time with them. At that time it would have been unusual, to say the least, for someone of my age. And there was the same old problem of there not being enough pocket money to make journeys just when you felt like setting forth. I still relied on my parents for money and they would need to know where I was going, and with whom. Without a doubt they would have refused permission. Almost certainly for boys there would have been more freedom, but not for girls.

With all this in mind I decided I should definitely go out and earn some money, find some sort of job in my holidays, which were just coming up. I will tell you about this spell of my life, Mukti, because you are at just that stage when you will shortly be searching for odd ways of earning money yourself. I looked up the small ads column of the local paper, went for interviews and eventually I was accepted for two jobs, neither requiring great skills. The first one entailed my parents buying me a small motorcycle called a Velocette – more elegant and more expensive than a Vespa, as well as less noisy. I needed it in order to trek across the moors to my first employment, which was doing housework and yes, cleaning, which unfortunately would include the dreaded dusting, in a pub that was absolutely tucked away in the wilds of Dartmoor, near Haytor.

The journey from home each morning was most enjoyable – lots of fresh air and speeding across glorious open countryside for half an hour, accompanied by a delicious sense of freedom. However, my occupation was not so salubrious on arrival, since it involved waking people up with cups of tea, who frequently hadn't quite managed to get themselves to bed in the first place. By which I mean, I would knock carefully on a bedroom door, and the knock would be answered by an agonized grunt. On entering the room, the grunting individual would as often as not turn out to be a man – single; it didn't seem to happen with couples – thrown carelessly and crumpled on to his bed, fully clothed. This state of affairs was known as 'the morning after the night before', and it seemed there were many of them. Pubs, I learned, were definitely for drinking in, and this one, being isolated and picturesque, was an ideal retreat for every sort of indulgence.

Then there was the cook, very old and pretty blind, who would pick up the dog's plate off the kitchen floor, over which she had just tripped, to arrange the guests' luncheon meat on it – not being able to see any other unoccupied dish. She would panic and woe betide anyone who tried to stop her, for she was very bad-tempered. Other staff were less eccentric – the head waiter taught me how to make a list and remember what people had ordered, how to entice the guests by telling them about the tasty things on the menu that awaited them (which was difficult when you knew about the dog's dish), and quite a lot about which wine went with what. It was an education, in its own way much richer than that offered by the finishing school. However, one day I arrived to find that things had gone too far. There was a terrible smell of sick when I entered the bar and smears of it on the floor, along with plenty of broken glass. There had evidently been some sort of party, followed by a bust-up, and not a single member of staff was around to explain what had happened. I went into the kitchen and that was empty too. The thought of clearing all this up was far too much of a challenge to face – I guessed it had been left for me – so I quietly slunk out of the back door, got on to my little motorcycle and sped off. So that, rather suddenly, was the end of my first attempt at earning a living.

My next little job was also short-lived. There was a tiny factory just on the edge of a nearby town which advertised for people to decorate the clay models that were manufactured there. It sounded interesting and slightly artistic. I went for an interview and found the job was not quite what I had expected. It was neither interesting nor artistic, but I accepted the job anyway as it was not easy to find employment at the age of seventeen, with no qualifications – just as it isn't easy now.

The function of the factory was to produce *objets d'art* for the tourist trade – gnomes and thatched Devon cottages, cups and saucers, jugs and small depictions in clay of a typical Devon cream tea. Each item had to have written on it a slogan or the name of a well-known place where it would eventually go to be sold. I was to be in the department that handled the writing on this assortment of oddities. Each object, once written on, had to be dipped into a vast tin vat of varnish placed against the back wall and then left to dry on a rack. I liked the look of the small crowd of people there, already busy at work. They seemed a cheery young lot and greeted me in a friendly manner, and there was an atmosphere of camaraderie. What I did find off-putting was the strong smell of varnish that filled the air. I wondered how they coped with it.

I soon found out when I started work the following week, for just as I had settled myself on a bench to do some writing, comments started flying in my direction:

'We've all got headaches. Bet you get one too.'

'Say if you start feeling faint.'

'People keep leaving because they can't breathe properly here!'

I was shocked. Why hadn't they all left? I asked. It seemed they were about to do just that, and it was hard for them because some really needed the money.

No sooner had I begun to get down to my writing – the name 'Ilfracombe' on the base of about a million gnomes lined up and awaiting attention – than I also began to feel strange. How can this be, I thought to myself, that people should have to work in such conditions? As it happened, after a few days and several trips to the head office to complain about the smell and its effect on our dwindling consciousness, we all walked out, the management having refused to do anything about the position of the vat of varnish. I didn't confess that the few hundred gnomes I'd dealt with, all had 'Illfracoombe' carefully inscribed at their feet. I always was a bad speller – something that Habib found strangely endearing. Somehow, I don't think the management would have felt the same.

I wanted to tell you these stories, Mukti, to give you an idea of how different conditions were then, but also to establish in your mind a better understanding of my life into which the relationship with Habib was slotted. Otherwise you might begin to think that my entire time was spent dreaming away and writing letters to your elusive grandfather and waiting anxiously for his replies, which would be enough to send anyone into a state of dreary torpor.

So these two jobs were my earliest attempts at earning a living. Compared to nowadays, there was a sort of haphazardness about lots of aspects of life. In this part of the world, health and safety regulations are so much tighter now and the workforce has a louder voice. That kitchen in the pub couldn't now be run like it was, and the fumes in the factory-cum-shed would be reported and an inspection would surely follow. And that is a good thing.

You have said that you think travel is very different now from when Habib set out on his great journey – that it is scarier these days, and that it wouldn't be possible to just wander around Europe picking up jobs here and there, as he did. I think it's certainly true that, especially in the case of Indians, it was easier then. For an Indian to come over to Europe now has become much more difficult, with visas ever harder to obtain and more expensive. Now, as you know, immigration and how to control it, is an important issue, which it wasn't in the '50s. In fact, it was encouraged then, and many people, quite apart from students, were actually invited to come to live in England from all over the world. The idea was that they would swell the workforce and help rebuild the country after the devastation of the war years. Many of them had a very tough time, often encountering the racism that was rife in England then, together with having to accept horrible jobs that no one else wanted to do.

However, for us Europeans it was much more difficult to get about. The Iron Curtain was a very real barrier to travel in the countries of eastern Europe, and I never heard of anyone getting to Russia. Spies did, of course, but not ordinary people. And Habib did. He writes about spending months in Moscow working on a film for which he was generously paid but which also bored him stiff. At the time, Germany was divided into East and West, and the East was out of bounds for the rest of us. But he got there too and stayed for many months. When we Westerners did go on holiday to other countries of Europe, we could only take £20 with us. That was the limit. Consequently, like many others, our family would go with our cousins to spend a couple of weeks by the English seaside during the summer, at the most.

In everyday terms, I can see that the world does feel more frightening now just to be in, let alone travel in, wherever you are. There is the drug scene for a start, which I can't remember hearing much about in the '50s. Drugs were always used by a few, certainly, but the habit was kept very quiet. Alcohol abuse seems to be a huge problem in all the countries of the West, and the media makes sure we all know about it. Likewise, child abuse, which appears to be universal. And of course, there is terrorism, the unexpected attack. My feeling is that life was slower and less complicated when I was growing up and, yes, it did feel safer. But that may have been because we simply didn't know as much about what was going on. When we did know, about the Cuban crisis for example and the very near catastrophe of nuclear war, there was much to be terrified about. But more often than not, our time was spent in happy ignorance.

We did not have the same material expectations as people have today. There was not that pressure because there simply wasn't the stuff around to yearn for. England was post-war by only a few years. It was a matter of doing without and getting by for most people, and you needed plenty of resources within yourself to keep afloat. Austerity was an overriding factor of the '50s. There were no 'fancy' things like computers or mobile phones around the home, because they weren't yet invented. Phones were there but I for one didn't use them nearly as much as I do now, since they were expensive and the reception was often poor. I certainly didn't think of phoning abroad unless there was an emergency. Even then, I still didn't necessarily lift up the phone because there were telegrams to send. Communication was so very limited compared to today; letters were definitely its mainstay.

Food was also different – much less variety and no freezers to keep it in. Most food was either tinned or fresh. So much that one takes for granted now had never been heard of. Pasta, for example, upon which most people are brought up nowadays. What was it? The nearest you got to it was through the kind intervention of Mr Heinz, who tinned it together with a very thin runny tomato sauce. It came on toast for tea and it was delicious. At least we thought so. Ready-made foods didn't exist in the sort of packages you get today, so if the housewife couldn't cook, the prospects for the family were dismal. Luckily, my mum was a very good cook.

You wonder what we did in our spare time, without the technology you are so used to, but for entertainment there was actually a lot of choice. Not being hooked up to a computer did leave much more time for activities at home. My recollection is that young people went in for making a lot more things than they do now. If you were a boy you constructed sophisticated models using delicate balsa wood and glue – things like ships, and planes and gliders that actually flew. There were Meccano sets of metal strips that could be bolted together to make a great variety of functioning toys ranging from submarines to cranes and tractors. If you were lucky enough, you might possess a scale model train set, which included the rails, several stations, tunnels, signals, even model trees and rolling green countryside. But you would probably need to wind everything up before it could work, and even then it didn't go for long!

Both boys and girls went in for collecting things – I collected stamps avidly when I was not yet ten years old but then lost most of my interest in them. Unfortunately, that is the reason why so many of Habib's wonderfully decorative envelopes coming from rare places are often missing their stamps. They were begged off me and I stupidly gave them away. I regret it now that I understand why people wanted them. The stamps were often lovely, like tiny paintings with every colourful detail perfect. They should have stayed on their envelopes – that's for sure.

For whole families to entertain themselves together, many of the same board games – Monopoly, Snakes and Ladders,

Ludo – were popular. They were not considered too tame even for grown-ups to play and, there being barely any black-and-white television, we played a lot. In fact, some of the more serious participants of any age in my family could become decidedly worked up if they were losing or felt that someone had cheated. I remember that tempers would fly about noisily on such occasions, people would stomp off and boards cleared with an angry sweep of the hand.

As a girl, I did a lot of crafty things at home like embroidery and crocheting. Mukti, I know you'll wince hearing this because it sounds so out-of-date, but I knitted as well, as I still do. And it was not just grannies and not just me – loads of us knitted because it was economical and fun to make our own garments. At that time most girls and women also made their own clothes from flimsy paper patterns which got spread all over the floor. You can still buy those patterns, but I don't know anyone who does. As a daughter I also helped in the kitchen with the cooking (on an ancient stove fed with coke), which is how most girls learned something of the art before leaving home.

One occupation of those days that seems to have all but disappeared is mending. It wasn't exactly amusing – stitching and darning, and glueing things back together when they broke – but it was oddly comforting, and I did a lot of it. I suppose I enjoyed it because it gave me the feeling I was in control of things I could understand, which I certainly don't feel now with so much that is digital or electronic.

Apart from writing copious letters and keeping a diary (which many people did), of course we read books. Compared to today we read masses. But the choice was not so wide, for there weren't nearly as many books written specially for young people. I would guess that even more so then, a book could have a huge effect on your imagination, on your life for that matter, and it was through my reading of Kipling's Mowgli stories when I was aged nine that I first became interested in India. The edition I was given as a birthday present had the most wonderful illustrations, very dramatic and colourful, as well as a beautiful text that I would pore over. The last illustration at the end of the story was of Mowgli in a village setting: he sat by a small white house with mango trees all around, together with his young wife, who was clad in a simple sari, and their baby son perched on his knee. It brought the feel of India very close and, when eventually I went there, it seemed extraordinarily familiar, no doubt because of my very early encounter with those beautiful images.

Apart from books, comics were an enormously popular source of reading. Political correctness was not much in evidence in the '50s; had it been, many of the characters that haunted our imaginations would not have survived such scrutiny; Rockfist Rogan for one, who pursued and vanquished the Huns on a weekly basis, Desperate Dan who could lift a cow with one hand and ate a disgusting dish called 'Cow Pie' for breakfast, and many other rogues and desperadoes who we loved. When we were children a selection of these comics, the Dandy, Beano or Champion, whatever we had ordered, would occasionally turn up in the post, by chance on the same day as the monthly sweet ration became available. This was a glorious day indeed, when you could lose yourself in a comic at the same time as consuming all of your three quarters of a pound of sweets in one go.

Radio was wonderful then as it still is, and with television only starting up in the evening, we listened to a lot of what was called "*The Home Service*. Some of the comedy programmes were very funny and skilful, like *Much-Binding-in-the-Marsh*. It was excellent and would hold its own for humour in any era. There is even some talk of re-broadcasting it. And there was an exciting programme about a detective called *Dick Barton – Special Agent* that I used to race home from school to listen to. I heard its theme tune just recently on Radio 4 during a discussion about its possible revival. It gave me the same tingle of anticipation as it had then.

Going out to the cinema was a great experience and there were some classically good films, films that literally opened your eyes to entirely different worlds – *Rebel Without a Cause* with America's 'first teenager' James Dean exploding angrily in colour on to the screen, the darkly brooding *A Streetcar Named Desire* with Marlon Brando as an icon of contained rage and, in a lighter but equally memorable vein, Elvis Presley immortalizing his first single hit song ballad '*Jailhouse rock*' in *Love Me Tender*.

Quite a few such famous films did the rounds in the bigger towns, but our village had its cinema too. It was called The Rex and was actually a large hut with a tin roof. When it rained you could barely hear what might be happening on the screen, but lovers kissed audibly in the back row – 'necking' or 'canoodling' we called it – and just about everyone rustled sweet papers, so there was by no means the deathly quiet you might expect today. It also leaked in places. The seats were hard and the films mostly in grainy black and white, but it was nevertheless an excellent way to spend an evening. After the show we would go and queue up for fish and chips at the local shop. It would be wrapped up in newspaper, sprinkled with lots of salt and vinegar, and shining with grease. Luckily for us, we were not nearly so health conscious as people are now in relation to food.

Dancing was another teenage occupation that offered a good opportunity for boys and girls to meet. People from all walks of life dressed up to go dancing. It was called 'ballroom dancing' and it is still a popular pastime amongst the seriously old-fashioned. In the village close to where I grew up there used to be dances held in the village hall. These could be gruelling occasions. The actual dancing was fine but in order to get a partner – if you hadn't come with one (and most didn't) – all the girls lined up on one side of the hall and all the boys on the other. You would have hated it, Mukti, and would have thought it quite barbaric. They would then eye each other uncertainly, while someone in charge would search for a suitable record to be played on the gramophone. Just before the music started some of the boys would sidle over to the girls' side to choose a partner attractive enough to dance with. It was a terrible fate if you were not chosen. You then became a 'wallflower' – and everyone could see you had been left on the side because nobody wanted to dance with you. I, for one, anticipated that happening with considerable dread, and I'm quite sure I was not alone.

Overall, I guess we had to make a lot more effort to keep ourselves amused in the '50s. But I don't think that did us much harm. On the contrary, it probably helped to make us stoical and more easily pleased.

So Mukti, there you have a brief outline of the times in which to place my life and Habib's letters. Now we need to get back to them to see where he is and what's been happening to him.

c/o Grindlays Bank,
54, Parliament St., S.W.1
Belgrade
26/8/56

My dear Jill,
Your prophecy seems to be coming right. It doesn't seem possible yet to go to the moon, but in a day or two I am going to Budapest.

I loved Italy, but more than that I like the landscape of Yugoslavia and the warmth of its people. I have seen many interesting places and met many interesting people here in the course of the last 2 weeks and I hope to be able to come back.

Coming to Edinburgh or England in the near future seems impossible now. I may follow the northern route to Berlin – i.e., via Prague and Warsaw. But I just don't know my programme. It depends entirely on money. I have none. I have finished all my continental quota for this year. I will go wherever I have prospects of making money. The trouble about these eastern countries is that you can't take any money out, though you can easily make a lot. I sang Indian folk songs for radio stations here and wrote many articles for newspapers and made a lot of money, but I must spend it all here or leave it and come back to spend it later.

But don't you think that I might disappear altogether or travel to New Delhi by land route. Come back to London I shall. When I cannot tell.

Are you positively going to Edinburgh? Tell me all about it if you do. And don't miss 'Henry V' and 'Oedipus Rex' in Stratford (Ontario Company of Canada)!

And how are you darling? And how and where is Carley? Remember me to your parents if you will. And accept my warmest love and a heap of kisses.

Yours, Habib

P.S. Thanks for your charming photos and all your lovely letters. Why the hell did you not sign the snap?

Six weeks had passed before the next letter arrived, by which time Habib had got well and truly into his travels. Hanging around waiting to set off had been irksome, as it always is, and despite the assortment of hazards already encountered, his tone is buoyant. In fact, your grandfather was one of the most resourceful travellers one could come across, thriving on challenges that would have immobilized most people. In truth, he almost seemed to invite them, to the extent that even the possibility of becoming destitute didn't throw him. That never quite happened, but he later describes some very close shaves. When I asked him, at the age of eighty-four, if he intended to keep on travelling, the answer was, 'Of course!' And when the question was extended to, 'And where do you want to go?' his reply was fervent: 'Everywhere!'

I missed him certainly and the idea of going up to Edinburgh to stay alone in the same house where we had been together the year before was daunting. That first visit to the Festival had been so intense; how could a second visit possibly live up to it? As it happened, it didn't. I don't remember much about that lonesome journey – what I saw or what I did. There had been such a strong sense of recognition in the very first moments of our meeting that it haunted my stay. Here, so obviously, was the same house, in the same setting, and the season was autumnal, just as it had been before – therefore Habib must be somewhere close by ... I would occasionally glimpse someone in the street who looked like him in some way, from the back, or the side, and would desperately want to follow them, just in case. It was an odd feeling, for I knew they weren't him on one level, but I could not help wanting to make sure on another.

There is *The Cockney Amorist*, a poem that tells of such an experience much more eloquently than I ever could, and it is by John Betjeman, written in the '60s. Here is its absolutely right final verse.

> I will not go to Finsbury Park
> The putting course to see
> Nor cross the crowded High Road
> To Williamsons' to tea
> For these and all the other things
> Were part of you and me.
> I love you, oh my darling,
> And what I can't make out
> Is why since you have left me
> I'm somehow still about.

Surprisingly enough, I too was 'somehow still about', and, in fact, had much to take my mind off Habib and his travels. For the next stage of my life was fast coming into view – and it looked very enticing and, what's more, apt. I longed for it to commence. For Habib too, this was a liberating and productive spell – he was in the thick of things, which suited him entirely.

Budapest
24th Sept' 56

My darling Jill
You complain you don't get letters from me; whereas actually I should be complaining. I got your letter of the 27th Aug. today. But since then you must have received my letter, probably from Yugoslavia, in which I have acknowledged your very, very sweet, smiling snap. I have tried to give you a smile back, though it is horrible. I hope you like the photo. This is the best acknowledgment and more concrete of yours. (By the way, why the hell didn't you sign the thing? – excuse the language – you see I have become a continental. I am even staying in a hotel called the Continental. And after all I am travelling everywhere.)

Do be patient, Sweetiepie, and you will get the contact back. I am travelling in difficult countries under difficult circumstances, and it is difficult even for me to keep track of myself. People here know the meaning of the word efficiency as little as I know my next address nowadays. And both these circumstances make it doubly difficult to keep in touch with anyone in the world outside. Give your letter a month, close your eyes and post it in the good name of Grindlays and you are sure it will get to me some time in life. Though by the time a letter containing a sweet youthful sentiment like yours gets to me, I feel much older. But never mind. And take a kiss for that, and another for your awfully sweet epistle, and yet another for your lovely snap.

What the devil am I doing here? Yes, that is a pertinent question.

Suffice it to say that I have seen not less than 18 plays in the last 3 weeks and met an even greater number of actors, writers and producers, and discussed many common theatre problems with them in relation to what I concretely saw of their work, most of which was familiar to me through translations.

I do not want to return unless I have seen theatres in Berlin, Moscow, Vienna, Amsterdam and Munich but of course I cannot tell. I haven't a penny now and can't get any from London, so I must earn and travel. I have succeeded so far, but how far more I will remains to be seen. That keeps me very busy writing articles and of course singing strange wretched Indian songs. I will leave Budapest soon but when and for where I do not know as yet. All that makes my plans uncertain and fluid. I do not expect to return to London before December; but then on the other hand, I may be forced to do so as early as next week for all I know. Of course I am bound to return and will let you know in due time. For I simply must see you again no matter what Herculean obstacles I have to overcome for doing that. 'GANGA', a film in English in which I play a small role is to be released here from today. I too am sorry not to have seen you in Edinburgh – I missed it when I read reports of it. I am glad you enjoyed it though. Won't you go back to school now?

Remember me to Carley and write everything about your present activities, though they are bound to become activities of the past by the time I get to know them. With lots of kisses, my dearest, dearest Jill.

*Your own,
Habib*

I was amazed and full of admiration for his resourcefulness in earning money in Europe. I wonder if one could do that now – simply going along, fending off one crisis after another with little earnings here and there? To add to his adventures, he was in Hungary just as the Hungarian uprising was about to boil over.

As for myself, I was preparing to go to Dartington College of Arts. I want to tell you a little about the place, Mukti, because, happily, it still features in our lives. I knew it then to be a very beautiful ancient estate, for I had been there for a singing audition some months before. Its history is interesting and I was very drawn to the Indian connections.

The poet Rabindranath Tagore was the fountainhead of its inspiration, but long before he came into the picture Dartington had stood for ages as an elegant manor house with a grassy courtyard, set in the midst of fertile Devon countryside. Built in 1388, it passed through several aristocratic hands including that of the Crown, until it was bought by Sir Arthur Champernowne, vice-admiral under Elizabeth I. The Champernowne family lived there for three hundred years, until the estate was purchased by Leonard and Dorothy Elmhirst in 1925, by which time it was more or less derelict. The gardens were medieval and you could well imagine knights jousting on the lawns overlooked by a solidly reclining Henry Moore figure. The whole place breathed history. This enterprising couple restored the buildings with complete generosity and breadth of vision over many years. It is through them, in particular through Leonard's friendship with Tagore and frequent visits to Santiniketan, that the Indian influence came in. Like Santiniketan, Dartington became established as a centre for progressive education with particular emphasis on the arts. It also engaged in rural reconstruction through its farms and land development. I couldn't wait to go there to begin my musical studies.

Meanwhile, I liked the idea of closing my eyes and posting off letters to Habib 'in the good name of Grindlays'. Grindlays Bank – it has a decidedly Dickensian ring to it. I imagined it tucked away in a dusty London side street, the entrance nondescript and sombre. Inside there would be many figures grinding away at their sums and accounts, little old men in dark suits with white faces carefully storing away Habib's letters, including mine, as they heaped up. Eventually, but taking their time, a nameless individual would totter down the road to post off one big packet – and how exciting for the recipient when it arrived.

Indeed, given the irresolute nature of Habib's movements together with frequent changes of address, they did very well to get anything to him at all. Grindlays doesn't exist any more. I think the name was all wrong for the present day.

Radehaul
6th December '56

My dearest Jill,
Radehaul is a lovely spot just off Dresden in East Germany, where I have come for a fortnight after spending 10 days

in Berlin. I will go back to Berlin from here and live there for another 10 days or so. I think I will turn back my steps some time early next year and perhaps be in London say by February 1957, when I do hope to see you again – grown more beautiful than ever perhaps.

I had left Budapest barely a week before trouble broke out there. I was there for 6 weeks. And in the beautiful towns of Czechoslovakia I spent five lovely weeks. My next destination from Berlin I do not as yet know. Perhaps Prague again and Paris.

Your account of your environment sounds good. I am glad you like it for once. I am expecting your latest letter perhaps written ages ago in the next parcel of letters from Grindlays in Berlin. I sent them my address only last week.

I think I simply have to wait in London indefinitely till my route to India is cleared. That might mean I have to look for a job and think of settling there for some time. That would mean I will see lots of you. Thrilling!
With all my love,

Yours, Habib

Where is Carley? And how? Remember me to her.

The news coming from Hungary was still seriously bad – and confusing. Had he not shifted when he did, Habib would have probably been stuck there for months right in the middle of a freezing winter. It was common knowledge that although Hungary was a communist country at the time and had its own government, it was nevertheless dominated by Russian policies and Russian secrecy. Much of the details of the uprising were not open for discussion until as late as the 1980s, when relations began to be more relaxed between eastern Europe and the West.

Basically, what is now referred to as the Hungarian Revolution started as a spontaneous gesture by students (many of whom had become Habib's close friends), and its aim was to oust the communist-led government that had been ineffectually in force since the war. It was nationwide and violent, lasting from 23 October 1956 until 10 November. In its final moments Russian troops invaded Budapest and, as a result, 2,500 Hungarians and 700 Soviet soldiers lost their lives. About 200,000 Hungarians subsequently fled the country as refugees. By 1957, the new Soviet-installed government had stamped out all public demonstrations.

By way of complete contrast, I was by this time finishing my first term at Dartington. I would have described it in my letters glowingly. It was just wonderful to be there and I felt very lucky. There lay ahead of me two whole years of artistic training in a gracious, ancient place with a serene atmosphere. The staff were mostly friendly and open-minded. They could enjoy their chosen teaching subjects without being under too much pressure of work, for there were, after all, only twenty-four of us studying music and about the same number of art and drama students. The learning groups were therefore very small. There were seventeen gardeners at the time, employed to make the environment glorious, which they did, and we had hours to spend wandering outside in the lovely open spaces and dreaming our dreams, which had never been possible for many of us before. I had an L-shaped bedroom all to myself that looked on to the courtyard, into which I could disappear to read or study or just be on my own. Even during the day there was time for that. To top everything, the food was good! It all added up to total happiness.

There were no exams to work for at the end of the two years, so you were free to soak up what seemed most useful to you according to your ambitions. We gave performances and shows from time to time and that could be stressful, but they were called Open Practice and were largely informal. Some wonderful visitors came to stay – singers and musicians of great renown, like Peter Pears and Benjamin Britten. And, amazingly enough, Ravi Shankar played for us more than once. We could talk to these exceptional people as friends because they ate in the dining hall and mixed with us. I think they all liked staying at Dartington because it was so peaceful and beautiful.

My spell there established in me a lifelong interest in learning and in education generally. When I think of those two years, I recognize that this was a very privileged environment, but that nevertheless some of its characteristics could be replicated elsewhere in other schools and colleges. The good food, for example. This is not more expensive to produce than bad food, if the ingredients are chosen carefully and the cooking is skilful. Then, the decoration of the rooms, which was utterly simple, mostly plain white, with cotton or wool curtains and plain floors of wood or stone. I am amazed at how ugly many places of learning are, as I have taught in many schools since then, and it is often not a matter of expense. Surely it is most likely that everyone can learn more freely if there is something of beauty to appreciate in the surroundings? Could it be that there is still the notion dating back to the Victorian era, even if unconscious, that children and young people need to be subdued by a dull environment? Why, otherwise, are schools too often ugly?

I think that Habib would have agreed with these sentiments. He cared enormously about education and could not fathom why it needed to be undertaken so arduously, often in dreary surroundings. Visiting the villages around Raipur in his childhood, as he frequently did, he much loved the simplicity of design and the colours of materials that he found there. His own shows reflected this simplicity and brightness.

We used to discuss these matters when we were together and I think our letters were beginning to settle into sharing what really mattered to each of us. There is a deepening of meaning as they go along, no doubt the natural effects of time and distance on the mind. An image of winemaking comes to my mind when I think of this – a fermentation process where the sediment gradually separates and sinks, leaving what is left altogether clearer and richer. I rather wonder if the same thing could happen if one were using emails to communicate? It's hard to imagine that their quickness would allow for such a satisfyingly slow process.

3

Berlin
22nd December '56

My dearest, dearest Jill,
You have become a lovely letter-writer darling. I was so very glad to read your letter. It was really awfully

interesting. It is a pity I cannot repay you by an equally interesting letter. For my mind is all in a muddle due to many problems – not the least of them being money. I must sit down right away and write some 3 long articles. And it is 1 A.M. Just now. It is a temporary problem, which recurs now and then; but I must solve it by tomorrow; for day after I go to Schwerin, a tiny little town in North Germany to spend Xmas with a friend. I am looking forward to it for I have heard that Germany has always been THE place for 'Xmas. I come back to Berlin on the 26th. I shall leave again for New Year's Eve to be spent with another friend in another little town in the South of Germany. I shall return again to Berlin on the 2nd Jan. perhaps for a day, perhaps for a week. What a dull reportage!

Thanks such a lot for a most exciting greeting card. It was so artistic and so appropriate – both for its picture and its greetings in many languages. (I am a traveller you see, for the last 6 months, of many lands.)

And you must believe me when I say that the card I sent you is about the best you can get in East Berlin, and I have only East marks. (And of course I sent 104 cards.)

I got your letter today and am replying forthwith for I expect that though am busy now, I shall get more and more busy day by day, as I am trying to earn enough marks not only to live here much longer, but also to be able to save enough and buy an open date ticket for flight to India from here. You see I can't sail any more because of the Suez. I have not enough money in London to take a plane. So if I can do it here, I shall be able to visit London with greater ease of mind and purse – then I can come back here later to take my plane.

I am very glad today, I got your letter. And I met 2 Hungarian friends from Budapest. Very good ones too. I have dozens there and very dear ones. And I have been writing letter after letter to find out about their welfare. I am glad they are all alive – each of them, though not everyone of them is in Budapest.

You are right about the Devon scarf most probably. I never got it. And I am sorry. It is entirely my loss and a great one. By the way it was a wonderful expression you used about the tank.

I am so very glad, Jill darling, that you are in Dartington. I have heard such a lot about it. In fact, had it not been for my leaving the Bristol School after the second term I would have spent half a term in Dartington as others did. I know it is a charming little place. I wish on my return I could visit it and see you in your new setting. In return – I wish for you that you could visit Tagore's own school of the same type generally speaking, in SHANTINIKETAN near Calcutta in India.

I was pleased, very pleased to hear you enjoyed Indian music so much.

And I was not a little surprised. For Indian music is so different from European, isn't it? Ravi Shankar is one of our topnotchers in Sitar. I was surprised he was there. You should have spoken to him about me. He is a friend. He had something to do with the music of a play of mine in New Delhi.

I am thrilled by the Berlin theatre especially Brecht's Berliner Ensemble.

I am seeing lots of them. I don't like Berlin as such, not as a city – it is too vast, a little graceless and empty. It is all bombed out you see. But I like many other things here. And I do like the average German – the common man and artists. Feel yourself kissed wherever you like with great love,

from,
Habib

Habib's long stay in Germany was possibly the most rewarding and the happiest time in all his travels. His 'ten days in Berlin' grew into eight months and he later returned there before going back to India. It was in Berlin that he immersed himself in the plays of Bertolt Brecht and that rich experience was to blend with his own thinking very positively. He found that many aspects of Brechtian theatre corresponded with his own. The inclusion of music and songs which had intrinsic value in themselves, the emphasis on down-to-earth language used by ordinary people and the underlying intent to make people think, even to shock them – these elements were familiar, and were already included in his 1954 Delhi production of *Agra Bazaar*. He observed that though Brecht's work was innovative, it was still essentially German, derived from the roots of his own culture. The observation was important, as it neatly reinforced ideas concerning his own position as an artist, about which he wrote later: 'I was clear in my mind that culturally I belonged in India. If you're dealing with words and culture you belong where you come from, because that's where you'll be your most creative.'

Disappointingly, the great man himself had died just weeks before Habib's arrival in Berlin, but his productions were there and so were many of his renowned actors and actresses. When he returned, Habib told me he had met them all, including Elizabeth Hauptmann and Helene Weigel, Brecht's leading lady and wife, and how enormously exciting and stimulating these meetings had been.

He also made some tremendously good friends – Rosie (Maria Magdefrau), who remained in touch even to the last year of his life when she accompanied him to the house where he was born, and Hanning and Cora Schroeder whose house he shared. He was surrounded by like-minded people with whom to discuss many things of common interest over many months and his accommodation was superbly suitable. He recalled it happily: '(The Schroeders) gave me a room in a lovely cosy attic – till today, that attic is always there for me. I'd get up in the morning, have breakfast with them and leave for the day for the East. I also saw a lot of West Berlin theatres, but the best theatres at that time were all in the East, drawing audiences from all over the world.'

My own time at Dartington was proving to be wonderfully interesting as well. In my letters, I would have written very enthusiastically about Indian music, for I found Ravi Shankar's performance riveting. It didn't seem to matter much that we student listeners were pretty ignorant as to how exactly the music came about, how it was structured and on what principles. The visual impact of the musicians was so clear and strong. The expressions, the movements, the concentration and the joy to be found in the rhythms and notes – these were universal, and enough to guide us into a remarkable amount of appreciation, considering it was the first time we had encountered live Indian music.

Meanwhile, I had taken to knitting a jumper for Habib in a beautiful bright blue and was very excited about it, since it was a huge undertaking for a not-very-good knitter and I thought it could reach him before the winter was over. I think I'm a bit obsessed even now with people being warm enough, especially when abroad, and well fed. I certainly was then, and had posted off one scarf to him in Hungary already, but I guess the post went quite haywire during the uprising, and he never got it. Hence my comment later on – which he liked – that it might have got itself wound around the gun turret of a tank, a possibility I found quite easy to imagine!

To my great consternation, after that letter of December, I never got another word of news for six months from Habib. I didn't even know where he was. By the time I heard from him it was the middle of June the following year.

Schroeder Berlin-Zehlendorf,
Quermatenweg 148
Krakow 19.6.57

My dearest Jill,
Can you once more forgive me? I got all your letters only 2 weeks ago upon my arrival in Warsaw after a sojourn of 6 months in Germany. I never thought I would be so long in that Country. I could not see my programme beyond ten days hardly. The result was that I asked my bankers in London as early as December 56 to send all my mail to my Warsaw address, where I then expected to arrive any

day. All of my letters waited me there all these months. They were 46. But not one of them was from home. That makes me a bit anxious. My mother is old and ill. It is monstrous of them not to write to me whatever might have happened.

No, I was not just having fun in Germany. I was working hard not only for a living but for an air ticket to Bombay. That took such a long time. But I have an open-date ticket now in my pocket at last. I can fly from Berlin any time up to April 1958. So I am carefree now. And I can travel about more calmly. I can even get this date extended if necessary. Perhaps it would be necessary.

The other achievement of this wretched struggle was, apart from many articles, mostly silly, a novel, which I think is not so silly.

I have undertaken to produce 2 Indian classics here in Poland next winter – 'Shakuntala' and 'Toy Cart'. That's good news, isn't it?

I shall be going to Denmark in July. I have taken an art course there.

Some time in July perhaps I shall come to London for a short time. If I cannot come then, I shall come some time in autumn for a longer period. In any case, I shall write to you about this and see if I should meet you in London or come to Devonshire to see you in your own setting. By the end of this month, I shall be back in Berlin and if your letter is to get me before the 5th of July, you might use the above address. From that date up to 21 July, I shall be at 'Hojskolen, VRA, Denmark' and after that my London address is as good as any.

Do forgive me. I was too busy. I was continually thinking of writing. I am full of remorse. But I am proud of that pullover, darling. No, I did not feel mean only. I also felt quite puffed up. No worthier cause deserves it. You will see when I get back to take it that I alone deserve it. Keep it please and do finish it if you haven't. I want to be in it to produce plays in Europe, and tell everyone interested who produced the pullover. A thousand kisses for it.

I went on a circular tour of this country from the sea to the mountains in the South. It is a lovely country. The people are very friendly. I am still working hard but earning much money.

It is more than a year since I saw you. You must have grown into a big girl now Jill. I am dying to see you. How are you going to spend your summer? Why not come somewhere in the continent and give me a chance to see you sooner?

I haven't the faintest idea about my programme after July. It depends entirely on replies to my many letters, including one from the Govt. of India. It also depends upon money – the amount I have, the kind of currency I shall earn, and the countries which are likely to provide possibilities for work. Of course I should like to choose those, which I have not seen.

When I see you next, I want to get you to sing for me. You were so mean you never gave me a chance.

I feel quite jealous of Ravi Shankar. He is a handsome man. Also a friend. He composed music for a play of mine.

Give my best belated wishes to Carley. How does she find the new house and life?

And how is your father now?

Have you yet forgiven me? Will you write to me soon and not be mean yourself and vindictive? I promise I shall never let you down again.
   With tons and tons of love and many many kisses.

God bless,
Yours as ever,
Habib

(PS) A few days ago I lost 2000 zloties – enough to live comfortably for a month in Poland. But I am being cheated of big sums of money in many countries. It is part of the fun of experiencing life abroad. HT

Grindlays certainly did have a hard task getting letters off to the right place. In this case they did their best, but Habib was not there to receive them, so they had obviously banked up even more than I had imagined, all forty-six of them.

I had got on rather slowly with my knitting, without the encouragement of news, and had got nowhere near finishing it. Now it being high summer, the current project, so painstakingly undertaken, would have to do for next winter. I clearly remember an occasion when I was knitting that jumper – in that lovely bright blue all-wool yarn. I was visiting my Gran at the time, in St John's Wood, London. We were in her sitting room, and she had looked at me thoughtfully from the chaise longue where she was reclining after supper and said: 'You know, that jersey is taking you so long that whoever it's for will have disappeared by the time you've finished it.' I could see her point and feared she might be right. Meanwhile, I wrote to Habib promising to send a replacement scarf for the one that had got lost on its way to Hungary. After his desperately long silence I also included a 'firm' resolution not to write him any more letters until I had heard from him.

Looking ahead, it seems that several things he mentions were destined not to materialize – the Polish production, the novel, the trip to Denmark – but perhaps this didn't matter so dreadfully, for his programme was always fluid. It had to be. What was important was getting that air ticket, and earning to keep going. I need to confess here that I never took Habib's money problems seriously enough. I did not have a proper idea of how hard it was for him to survive in the West or even, for that matter, back in India. With his precarious income, he couldn't count on a social security system or a national health service. We are so used to these support systems in England that we cannot imagine actually going hungry or being ill without help or treatment, because of lack of money. That this can happen Habib demonstrated more than once on both sides of the world. It taught me a great deal when he eventually sent a photo where he looked so thin that I was horrified. I wished I had had more understanding earlier.

I did get around to singing to Habib, incidentally. From time to time it happened, I'm glad to say. And the last time I sang for him was in Bhopal, even as late as 2006 – a gospel song in a friend's house, into which I injected a huge amount of feeling. He was moved and said, 'Your singing is *remarkable*!' He said it very solemnly, making it a real gift of a compliment.

Photographs of Habib (who had lost a lot of weight by then) and Jill. Their daughter, Anna, carried these photographs in her wallet for close to thirty years and they are rather the worse for wear

614, Hotel Ukrain,
Moscow, 18.8.57

My dearest Jill,
I again got your letter quite late, thought if I had received it earlier, I do not see what difference it would have made except that I would have replied earlier and felt a bit better for it. As it is, I am feeling quite wretched. Your letter had a sobering effect. It was touching. Thanks a lot darling for your lovely invitations and for the scarf which I now seriously believe I really do not deserve. Because again I do not know how long I shall be before I return to England. Your decision to write to me only when you hear from me is hard but reasonable. If you can relax it occasionally I shall be only too grateful for the mercy, as undeserved as the love expressed in your scarf.

Up to the middle of October at least, I am quite sure I cannot come. I am working in an Indo-Soviet film here –

called 'Afa Nasi Nikitin' – the name of a Russian merchant who traveled to India in the 14th Century. I am Afa Nasi's Indian voice.

I attended the Youth Festival here – a gigantic affair. About five hundred Indians were here – among them many old friends, some of whom I met after many years. There are many Indians working here already not only in this film but in other spheres. So it is pleasant, all said and done. I live comfortably and earn a lot of money and spend it recklessly.

It is a beautiful summer – in Moscow. There is frequent sunshine. I take a cold shower twice a day.

Did you enjoy your holidays or did you spend it cursing me? I hope not for your sake. How is Carley and her groom? Remember me to them.

One day I will certainly return, Jill. I am not yet sure when that day will be. But I have one fear. I may return for a short period but you might be too busy to run up to London. That will be bad. That horrible prospect can however be done away with if we both promise to make supreme efforts. I promise. Won't you?

A kiss for the scarf and all that distant love cannot give.

Your own,
Habib

That I did not stick to that threat, not to write again unless I had heard from him, goes without saying. The charming plea for mercy that was Habib's response thoroughly undid my resolve. I'm glad it did, for, by and large, I'd rather risk feeling foolish for being soft than being heaped up with regrets later on for being hard. But it wasn't really a matter of feeling foolish either, for I enjoyed writing and would have deprived myself as much as him if I'd started rationing my output.

I also knew I had not made the 'supreme efforts' that I might have done to get to Europe. I was daunted by the prospect but could probably have worked harder at mitigating my fears. The truth was, I had got involved in my own life at Dartington by now and had another boyfriend, who had the huge advantage of being present. He was kind and attentive, played the violin like an angel and had red hair and freckles. He was called Robin, just like the bird, the redbreast. I liked him a lot and was very comfortable with him, but that is different from being in love, which it seemed to me I was not.

All the same, I did not want to be further divided. I was torn enough as it was, waiting for letters and thinking about Habib, without the feeling being reinforced by a brief meeting in some romantic corner of the world, which I knew he would almost certainly be leaving all too soon. And another possibility: perhaps he would not make it to the country where we'd have planned the rendezvous, in which case I would be stranded without the language and without the money to put myself up in a hotel. It was a real fear too, for as you can see, Mukti, plans were always changing.

Habib in Russia was not the same as Habib anywhere else. I notice now that the tone of his letters from Moscow were consistently slightly depressed and tired. He later described his work in the field of dubbing beautifully, bringing home to me how tedious and phoney it felt to him. Living well and earning well did not compensate for this. It was definitely a low point in his journey. I had no idea that Russia could attract and accommodate so many Indians when for much of the rest of the world it was forbidden territory. Having familiar faces and friends around must have been one cheering aspect at least, but the tone continues to be quite sombre. Westerners could not travel there, of course, because of the Iron Curtain. But I did promise to do what I so badly wanted to when he returned to England – which was to make those 'supreme efforts' for us to spend time together, however difficult.

614 Hotel Ukrain
Moscow 20.8.57

My dearest girl,
Thanks ever so much for your beautiful card and the fact that you wrote even before hearing from me. To your previous letter I replied only 2 days ago. That letter will show you that it is impossible for me to go with you to Ireland in September, much as I would love to do it. My film work would keep me here well up to October.

A kiss for your second invitation to Sanduck Farm, which too I am unable to accept. It pains me but it cannot be helped. Please darling, forgive me. I am sure, however that I shall be able to see you before I return to India. Perhaps in the autumn. I shall write.

No, I never went to Denmark. I went to some places in Western Germany instead. I had to do it some time. It was obligatory. So I am glad it is over. I went to Bayreuth, Lindan, Frankfurt, Bamberg and some other beautiful places. It was lovely weather and wonderful country.

My work is hard, and tiresome. I hope it comes to an end soon. The Moscow summer this year is simply superb. You would not wish for better weather.

I hope you are not getting tired of me Jill. Are you? I shan't blame you if you are.

Do write to me about Ireland and Carley. And don't forget to add a word about yourself. I should so like to see you. You must look different. It is such ages since I saw you last. I hope you are not taller though. You will simply grow out of me, if you grow longer.

*Lots of love,
Habib*

Only two days separate this letter from the one before, which is quite remarkable. It has a lonely ring to it still, and even the reference to visiting so many places in Germany doesn't lift the mood. Travelling so much, I guess there comes a time for everyone, no matter how dedicated, when it all appears tiring and somewhat pointless. It's a low point that will pick up, but at the time you don't see that – you just want to go home. Habib was pinned down now for months to come, and the work was boring. He'd been away for over a year from England and over two years from India – a difficult time.

Jill with her new short hair

My appearance had indeed changed but I don't think I was taller. All that had happened to me was that I had cut my permanent wave off – my curls were gone, and I had naturally straight hair again. It was more in keeping with the rustic ideals of Dartington; a perm would have been quite out of fashion, especially there. As far as growing was concerned, ever since meeting my sister Carley, I think Habib rather feared being drawn to an English girl who would tower over him. I was three inches shorter than her and just his height, at five feet seven. Anyway, I was eighteen by this time and not likely to be extending myself like a ladder, on and on! I loved the quaint idea that I would simply grow out of him if I grew 'longer'.

Another interesting diversion concerned Carley, who had recently got married. As you can tell, Mukti, I responded with some force to his suggestion that I write all about her and just add a word about myself! I was peeved at the comment – I guess I was jealous – and this did stir Habib enough to sound more like himself.

614 Hotel Ukrain
Moscow, USSR 5.9.57

My dearest Jill,
I have just received the sweetest of all letters from England, the warmest of all letters from a cold country, from the most warm-hearted girl.
I must have written that in haste – 'a word about yourself and a lot about Carley' – it does sound funny, it is so enormously rude. Anyway, I am really and truly glad you wrote about yourself at length and with such lyrical,

touching intimacy. Frankly I was also delightfully amazed – I have never known myself being able to draw out so much expression from you about matters of heart. Thanks such a lot for what you write you feel for me. Love has such wicked weakness for flattery. It is vicious that your sincerity, instead of sobering me only should make me also feel flattered. Yes it means a lot to me Jill darling and I shall remember your words always.

Jill, it seems to me I have gotten to know you much better in your absence. Ever since I began to receive letters from you after leaving England I have been longing to see you again. I feel certain I shall see you again. I am sad our meeting might be brief. I sometimes play with the hope it might be a bit longer and make all sorts of vague plans to be able to live longer in England. But I know no duration of time would be long enough.

The only consolation is the perpetual feeling that it is so wonderful to know you.

Do my words have a ring of farewell about them? Yes but every letter, every winged word that I throw up in the air for you must have this sad note. Your letters full of depth and richness of feeling have the same quality. But we shall meet before we say goodbye Jill.

I was very glad to hear about your voice and about your confidence. I think it is a good idea to go to Munich. It will be good for you for many reasons I think. I like Germany and Munich.

I get up at 7 a.m. For work and get back at 5 p.m. It is a bit much. It is hard to stand on your feet for so long, to see just one pair of lips projected on a screen in a darkened room continuously, to hear the same words and the same voice the whole day, to speak incessantly with feigned emotion before a machine, to laugh a 3 foot laugh then take a 4 inch sigh and rattle off a sentence of 3 foot 4 inch length of celluloid, to weep, shout and love in pre-measured lengths – often without food. This is dubbing work. I am losing weight fast enough. You can imagine. It will be a job for you finding me when I do return. I am expecting to become invisible within a matter of a week. I do hope all this comes to an end soon enough.

Thanks heavens, there was some sort of Jubilee which stirred the postal authorities of England to change their eternal dull stamps into something slightly less dull. Few other countries can beat England in this regard.

You are cheating you know. You may write the most interesting postscript in the world. But a p.s. is a p.s. and not another letter. For my second letter you write a p.s. you silly scoundrelly girl. And by now you will have got my card as well. You would find it indigestible unless you throw it up. Till we meet X

Habib

(Ps) I just poured some coffee in my ash tray and dropped the ash of my cigarette into the coffee cup. I have just washed them and now I drink the remains of the precious little coffee in a more conventional way. Love HT

Do send those photos but never mind if you have no space for Carley. Write a lot more about yourself. Yes, I had meant it

> *when I desired the culmination of our emotions in physical union. And I think we would have fared fine. Lots and lots of love from HT*

All of this letter moved me very much and still does – so expressive, serious and loving. It reminds me of autumn, with its 'dying fall'. What could those PSs have been about – mine, I mean? I simply can't remember, but I guess I was asking questions to which he responded in his last few lines – questions about love and in what way it could best be expressed. And what we were to do about it.

As a young girl with little experience, I was trying to feel my way, seeking reassurance. Evidently, there had to be a deciding moment in our relationship. How far was it to go? What degree of commitment could I bring to it? And where was he in these matters? We had discussed the future somewhat vaguely before he left for Europe, and had come to no conclusions. But whatever was said, there was always the fear he could go back to India, disappear without trace – the thought of which filled me with apprehension and uncertainty.

Writing these words has encouraged me to think more broadly on the subject of physical love, which of course had been a preoccupation for both of us. I have never believed that men and women are the same in their emotional responses in this respect. I know, Mukti, that it has become popular today to think there is little difference between the two, but I disagree. Biologically, men and women are certainly different and I believe those differences go very deep. One could say that there is no reason why a man shouldn't simply walk away from a sexual encounter whatever the outcome, whilst for a woman, there is the chance of her life changing forever. It may well not happen, but the possibility of creating another life is there in the very nature of lovemaking for her, and I don't believe that the various contraceptives available have allowed women to escape this fact. Our bodies and our psyches are still finely tuned to bearing children, whether we like it or not. That is what I sensed at a young age, for I certainly took the whole subject seriously. It made me cautious about how to approach such an important area of existence, though I doubt if I'd have been able to put the thoughts into words.

But you are right, Mukti: whatever I was pondering, this was becoming – already was – a love affair by letter. But the letters change in tone too, don't they, just as feelings change day by day in a love affair – sometimes full of deepest emotion, sometimes quite matter-of-fact. They carry their own life, quite palpably.

Looking back, I can say that despite being aware of many difficulties ahead, it was this letter that persuaded me to pitch into the knowing and the loving of Habib with all my heart, whatever the cost. From time to time life requires you, pushes you, into making a move that may look quite reckless and stupid to others. The challenge is that of jumping out of the realm of the known, into wherever it takes you. It seems that only a blind sort of faith is there to support you, but the sense of destiny is strong and it is that which gives you the push. I'm sure nearly everyone must recognize such a moment at some point in their lives. It comes as a watershed – and can change everything.

614 Hotel Ukrain
Moscow 27.9.57

My dearest Jill,
Thanks for a lovely letter and those wonderful photos. Carley certainly looks different now. And you look so charming when you are a bit screwy. I should like to see you a bit screwy when I see you again. You too look a little different – much more lovely still. And I was delighted to look at Sanduck Farm. How I wish I could be there. You are darned lucky. You have also a handsome brother. Who is really responsible for that?

Your letters give me very special joy. I am not quite myself in Moscow.

I am a little tired.

I am glad you will be in Germany in January. I am sure you would adore the snow there. The winter is a thousand times better here in the continent. For one thing, no fogs. For another, perhaps I ... Oh, I do wish I see you soon. I don't know where I would be in a month's time Jill. Perhaps India, perhaps Poland, perhaps London or Germany. Delhi wants me to look after a play which has been abandoned for the time being because the original producer is suddenly taken ill. She is told to take rest for some time. She has something wrong in the lungs. The play is Shakuntala – the theatre is my theatre called the Hindustani Theatre with the same initials as mine.

This theatre I had organized in Delhi before leaving India. This is the first professional theatre in Delhi. From last month it has started functioning as a semi-professional organization, to be soon turned into a fully professional venture. I cannot go to Delhi immediately as I am wanted but if they can wait till November I shall go to India with a return ticket from here for 3 months.

The letter you get from me in a month from now will certainly have a clearer picture of my programme.

South Germany is very picturesque. I like it very much. I also look forward to seeing my new girl soon. Gosh, you must have changed. You were a kid when I left you.

Lots and lots and lots of the best of love from

Your Habib

I do wish I had duplicates of those photos, for the mention of the 'screwy' look is most intriguing. I will just have to imagine how I managed to look both screwy and lovely at the same time.

I had sent pictures not only of myself but also of my family and the farm, and Habib mentions my brother Kevin, who was two years older than me. They had not yet met, but were to get to know each other quite well when Habib returned. I must say a little bit about your grand-uncle Kevin for he was exceptional, not just for being clever and handsome, but more than anything else, for being absolutely avant-garde in his tastes and his thinking. Come to think of it, you are quite like him in certain ways, Mukti. I guess it is because you are so modern and freethinking that you remind me of him, and you are definitely trendy, as Kev was; he also had the same sardonic humour as you. He was one of the first of his era to wear Edwardian jackets, and grow his hair long, for which he was teased unmercifully by some older members of the family.

One rather ghastly old relative called out to him quite rudely in the middle of a party: 'Kevin, your hair is so long you look like a girl.' To which he responded equally loudly: 'Well actually, I'm just in the middle of changing sex!' In the '60s, he got to know the Beatles, Mick Jagger and Mary Quant, the top icons of that extraordinary era, and set about starting the very first discotheque with the help of George Harrison, in London. You would have loved him, Mukti.

When they did meet, Habib and Kev got on well and enjoyed some intense discussions on the subject of modern-day trends and culture. Another long exchange I remember took place at the farm in Devon and that was about the significance of money in one's life. But Kev was not to last further than the '60s. Always a complicated and slightly unstable character, he got caught up in some of the more perilous aspects of that era, becoming involved in the drug scene that was virtually its hallmark. He died at the age of twenty-nine, leaving a jagged rent in the fabric of our family which could never be mended.

My brother Kevin

The sense of weariness that seemed to permeate Habib's stay in Moscow continued. I have never been there myself but the feeling I have is that life in Russia could be heavy going even to this day, especially in winter. Perhaps I have seen too many news clips, but my impression is of long, grey queues of people in front of the shops, muffled up against the cold, waiting endlessly for scarce provisions. It always looked a grey sort of place to me. Undoubtedly, being required to stay there to earn in such a tedious way and for so long, months and months, must have been extremely trying. Now there was India and emerging difficulties in the Hindustani Theatre that just could not be ignored. On top of these obstacles, a Russian winter is famous for its extremes of cold and there he was about to be in the middle of one with inadequate clothing. I had read about ferociously severe Russian winters in various novels and descriptions of the war, and I worried very much that Habib, always quite frail of build and a lot more so since leaving England, might not survive. How I wished that that jersey could be sent, but to me, Moscow seemed so remote a place muffled in snow that I couldn't imagine any small parcel reaching there. Nor did the local post office advise trying, and I didn't want the precious garment to be lost like the scarf. What a pity, for it was now finished and beautiful, the best and most perfect thing I had ever knitted.

My own hesitant plans were to spend some time in Germany to learn German, which is an important language for a singer, and to seek out a singing teacher who would take me further. To do this, I needed to find a family with whom to stay when I had finished at Dartington. That is why I was going to Munich in January. A German family with whom we had connections was happy to have me, but I remember not really wanting to make that journey. It was one of those occasions when a seemingly sensible progression of one's life comes into view, but for all its apparent propriety, it just doesn't feel right.

> Habib Tanvir,
> 614 Hotel Ukraine
> Moscow. 7.10.57
>
> Dearest Jill,
>
> Thanks for your beautiful card. Yes, I got the photos & loved them as I have already written. I am dying to see your new hair-cut, and also to touch, feel & kiss it.
>
> No, you sent me no stamps.
>
> It is awful cold here — something below zero. Br-r-r!
>
> My theatre in Delhi needs me. It started functioning but the producer (the only other producer apart from me) was suddenly taken ill & advised complete rest for some time. In the meantime, Poland wants me on 15 November for the Indian production. So I don't know whether I will go to Poland in November or India. I might return from India in May, if I go now.
>
> A third interesting complication is that some Budapest artists want me

> to join them, act pantomime with them and travel around in the world. I wait for some telegrams; then I decide — in about a week's time from now I think. There is still a chance that I come to London sometime in November — but for a very short time — due to financial position. And I must send my luggage from London. It is a pity that I neither have the time to be to earn money in London nor to spend as much as one would like to. However, I am bound to run up to see you when I come or get you in London if you can come. I shall write about my programme again soon.
> This darned drilling is boring. Curse it, when will it's end!
> A billion kisses.
> Jun
> Habib.
>
> Shall send new photo as soon as I get one. Maybe next week. H.T.

It was a disappointing time for both of us, with many plans in the offing but none of them secure. I was in just the same frame of mind, uncertain about everything, and trying without success to get excited about my German plans. Dartington would be coming to an end in a few months and some ideas had to be formed regarding the future. Perhaps the stars were in some sort of disorder and affecting both of us!

Later on in my life I had a good old friend in her eighties, called Rosemary, who was very well versed in astrology. She had a real feel for it and whenever I was going through a difficult patch, with things going wrong, I would ring her or pay a visit and ask her what was happening. She'd reel off complicated explanations relating to the movements of the heavens, complete with the names of planets, which so often seemed to be in such a muddle, and then tell me approximately how long the present disturbances would last. 'Don't try and make decisions for at least a fortnight,' she'd advise, or, 'Not a good idea to travel just now, Jill. You probably won't have a smooth journey.' And oddly enough, she was always right. I could have done with such guidance at this point, or advice from friends, but it wasn't around so I just had to keep going, stumbling around in rather a dark spot, much like Habib.

614, Hotel Ukrain,
Moscow,
13.10.57

My dearest Jill,
Got one of your loveliest epistles just now – all about wandering sheep, changing hues, falling leaves and ripening thoughts. No, seriously. If it is a joy for you to write to me, Jill darling, (and I am glad to hear it), it is a joy of equal measure for me, if not more, to read your thoughts. This particular letter contains shades as soft

and nice as autumnal leaves have – and it fills me with a longing to have a look at your pictures. I am sure they must be very nice. Have you got any miniature which you can conveniently send?

Do you mind? I never suspected you painted too.

And thanks also for that bit about Ravi Shankar. He is truly great. Did I tell you he wrote music for one of my plays? The article about him is very well written indeed. He was extremely popular here in the U.S.S.R. as well.

No, he is getting around much more than I, though I have not yet excluded China, Japan and America from my itinerary. In fact, I would do well to include the Moon too now, wouldn't I? I remember you predicted this. (I have written a poem on the Man-Made-Moon.)

I am not going back to India soon now Jill. I wish I was, because then I had a chance of seeing you in November. As it is, I must proceed to Poland now in order to produce the Indian Play. I decided this because of an invitation from a certain Budapest theatre to join them as a pantomime actor in January and travel along with them. It is a group of 3 – which includes me and a couple – which will undertake this trip. I do not know how long you will be in Munchen. Perhaps I shall see you there, if we go there – we might.

This means I shall be around here until about next August or so. Tell me; when do you propose to return to England from Munich?

If I do not see you until next summer Jill, then I would be seeing you after 2 years. Terrible. I don't like it one bit. So I am still trying. If the Polish theatre can wait a bit, I want to run up to London in November. But I have absolutely no hope, though I wait for their answer. You see they can perhaps wait for a few months but it might be difficult for them to wait for a few days or weeks – a difficult gap to fill in theatre. I hate my self-imposed helplessness.

For all I know I shall be leaving Moscow on the 8th of November. My work here is expected to finish before then. Poland wants to start production of the Indian play from 15th November.

I think your reply to this may be your last letter to me in Moscow.

Anyway, I should give my last letter a fair ten days' time. After that, please use my London address until I am in a position to send you my next address. But I shall let you have my Polish address as soon as my programme is a bit more settled.

Do let me know if you would be able to manage to run up to London for a few days, in case I happen to come in November. Where would you be in November? Please send me your telegraphic address (or addresses with dates) for November.

I met a delightful American author here. He has written books on Japanese and Indian theatres and travelled very widely – Fabion Bowers. His wife an Indian woman (a 6 footer), is a novelist. Between them they know half the theatre world of America. You can imagine what a valuable contact it can be.

With nothing less than love,
Your Habib

I had included with my letter an article cut from a magazine that was particularly interesting, about Ravi Shankar. By this time I had a sneaking suspicion that Habib was afraid of me falling for the handsome musician with whom he had collaborated in India. He just keeps mentioning him and repeating himself! In fact, it would not have been difficult, given the irresistible combination of Ravi's good looks and amazingly seductive playing. I'm glad to say, any temptation was removed as a result of his heavy schedule of concerts elsewhere.

I must have written about the autumn in Devonshire which included Dartington and the farm, both lovely places to be at that time of year. But I expect I wrote more about Sanduck Farm than anywhere else because it was such an important place for me. I will tell you a little about it, Mukti, because then you'll understand better my great passion for keeping chickens wherever I can – which, I gather, you find a little eccentric – and growing vegetables even in the middle of town.

This was a place we moved to when I was eleven years old, and the reason was that my father couldn't settle down or get a job after the war, and was sick and depressed. London didn't suit him, and the thinking was that tucking him away where there was plenty to do, deep in the Devon countryside, might resolve some of his problems. For me, hearing we were going to live on a farm was the most tremendous news. I had friends at school who were boarders but went back to their farms in the holidays and I had hardly dared to dream that this might one day happen to me. We spent most of that summer holiday touring around farms looking for the right one, finally settling on Sanduck. It did not answer my dreams in the sense that it was not old – it was built in

1902 to be exact, the year carved in granite over the front door – but it had the most wonderful atmosphere of space and separateness. It was, more than anything else, a sturdy place set in beautiful rolling landscape just bordering on the wildness of Dartmoor, with strong barns and buildings all around offering endless possibilities for use.

My granny had kept hens all along and after the war. One of my earliest memories of the time we lived with her was being taken to her vegetable garden and being told to lift the sloping lid of the henhouse nest box. There sat a hen almost the same colour as the golden straw beneath her. Putting my hand under that pale blonde feathery bird and gently pulling out from under her a warm egg was one of the most enchanting moments of my life. Strangely, she didn't seem to mind having her treasure removed, or want to peck me either.

From that day onwards I had a desire to keep chickens and here at Sanduck was an ideal opportunity. During my first school holidays there I immediately set about buying some hens – 'point of lay' Rhode Island Reds, they were called – and set them up in a small round and ancient Roman ash house that stood opposite the main house, making nest boxes for the arrival of their first eggs. They were purchased as castaways from a battery hen farm nearby, where they'd been imprisoned in small wire cages and could do nothing at all for themselves. On arrival, the hens fell out of their crate, wobbly on their feet and bald in patches where they'd had their feathers pecked off, either by themselves or other hens. Very quickly they grew strong and flourished, with plenty of fresh grass and space to roam over. Bit by bit they returned to their natural habits, like taking dust baths to smother any nits they might have, and scratching the earth to find grubs to eat. I sold the eggs to passers-by or down in the village. A great problem arose when any of these birds were very sick or very old and needed to be dispatched. I would get our cowman, Bill, to do what was necessary and run off while he was at it.

By the time the chickens were well established we had bought up a whole herd of black-and-white Friesian cows which arrived in lorries. The milking parlour was a clattering, banging sort of place in which those of us who worked could sing very loudly. The acoustics were perfect – the cows must surely have enjoyed the singing, and I believe it helped them relax while being milked. I was allowed to choose a calf to call my own and rear. I chose Valita, a very girlish calf with long eyelashes, born of one of the highest milkers in the herd, and spent a lot of time brushing her shiny pied coat. At other times we went in for goats, pigs, ducks and sheep, all of which supplied me with a variety of lessons in providence, far outweighing in usefulness anything I was learning at school.

Having to go back to boarding school three times a year was very difficult. You have not had to face boarding school, but I can tell you, at least for me, it was very nerve-racking to shunt between and try to adapt to two completely different life styles. Leaving all these fascinating creatures behind was particularly worrying, as I could not see how anyone would look after them as carefully as I did! It was only when I started at Dartington, which was relatively close by, that I could stop feeling that my life was chopped into uncomfortably short bits. I could get back home at weekends to carry on the thread of my farming activities and this is what I often chose to do.

Writing to Habib about the farm gave me great pleasure, and just as it was a delight to hear from him, it was also a delight for me to write to someone dear who responded so warmly and sensitively. Such appreciation gave me the confidence to share my very best and most lyrical thoughts, and at eighteen this was a wonderful outlet for so many new, intense feelings.

4

614, Hotel Ukrain,
Moscow, 7.10.57

My dearest Jill,
I just received your manliest letter so far – one of your sweetest actually. No one's letters make me feel compelled

to answer so instantaneously as yours do, with sheer love – an unspoken demand. I have replied to your Sanduck letter already, so I shall not repeat that I am not returning to India now. No, dearest Jill, I do not think I feel differently about our meeting. Your reaction to my plans of going to India is justified I think. But the call from Delhi was perhaps not so whimsical as you imagine. It was a question of prestige of the very first production of the first professional theatre in the capital, which I had myself helped to set up.

Thank heavens that the original producer, who had so suddenly fallen ill would be able to resume work in a few weeks, and meanwhile they have been able to get someone else to look after the rehearsals. (It is not easy to get good producers in India). Anyway, I am enormously relieved, because I too loathed the idea.

In November, however, I may yet not come, dear Jill. I doubt it extremely darling. It is not a question of money, which I have – nor of my wish, which too I have. I have both in good quantities. But time perhaps I may not have until January, though I promise you I am still trying to come to London in November because I long to see you Jill darling. But we can certainly meet during Xmas, if you come to Krakow instead of going to Munich. Honestly, can't you do that? Do let me know if you are sure to come to Europe during Xmas. How long will you stay, if you come to Munich?

The Polish theatre could wait till next May but they cannot put off their production for a few days or weeks – you see. Much depends upon when my film work finishes. But

I have no hope it would leave me any breathing space. It was due to be finished in September. Even if I get a week, I would fly to London. Or, I could come only after finishing my production in Krakow and before leaving for Budapest. But you might be in Europe then.

Your letter presented me a glimpse of the same mood you had on that day last year when everything was going wrong with us in London – no cinema, no good cafe – but it all turned out fine at the end. I am hoping for the same and in this case too.

But Jill, my dearest girl, do, do write to me your programme for Xmas and the next year, if you know it definitely.

I think you are right about the jersey. I should hate to lose it, even though I am not able to help myself to earn it.

You are worse than my mother, Jill, though this time even she is justified – what with the time I am taking in my journeys abroad and the time of life she has got left at her disposal now. But I love her the more for it too.

I too have been thinking much about this forced separation, my dearest Jill, or I wouldn't be writing so breathlessly. But I am sometimes inclined to philosophize it and think – well, what difference does it make when I simply must depart again. It does make a difference though. I want to see you in any case.

Keep your fingers crossed and pray that my work here comes to a happy or unhappy end quite soon.

With all the best of love, all its very best,

Your Habib

Your letter so full of love is so overwhelming. It is enough to make anyone run up to you, dear Jill.

I can't remember taking Habib's invitation to come to Krakow seriously. I suppose the thinking behind my state of mind was: Krakow! How on earth do you get there! And maybe Habib won't have reached Poland after all, as he often doesn't get to where he plans to go. Perhaps he would have been called back to India to rescue a production or to support a new theatre company. But there were also a few practical reasons which would have made me stay put. Still no source of money for serious travelling that wasn't provided by parents, and no one else who'd want to come with me; I'd have had to go by myself. Writing letters was a lot simpler, and after much practice I was becoming an expert in conveying all that I felt. So there, Mukti, I missed another chance of adventure – something that might be difficult for you to understand. I do think Habib showed great patience in constantly waiting for me to turn up and constantly being disappointed.

Eventually I did shift myself and made great efforts to travel to meet him so that at last he could 'run up' to me, but I had to wait until I was older.

Moscow 9.11.57

Dearest Jill
I have 2 lovely letters from you – dated 19 & 26 Oct. Thanks ever so much.

I think I have a much clearer idea of the Sanduck Farm now. And I am tempted to be there and get into that room with the striped curtain, smell all its perfumes and breathe its passionate air which makes you write such nice things. Your picture of it is very nice I think.

I really want very much to see some of your pictures and clay models and hear your singing, if you would be so good as to let me. I have a suspicion they must all be awfully nice. The way you feel about things – that sensitivity gives me this suspicion.

'Bhagavada Gita' is a very interesting book I think and so is 'The Discovery of India'. I have conceived and made the first rough draft of a play based on Gita's concept of action; 'Action is inaction and inaction action.' This was years ago. Some day I hope to finish it.

I am sure you would like the simplicity and lyricism of Gita and some of its thoughts too. And Nehru's book is a mine of information I think and extremely readable. No wonder you like it.

Child art has been likened by some with primitive art. They say there is much similarity of approach between the mind of a child and that of primitive man. Perhaps that is the reason why profiles are common in both the arts. You may be right therefore that they drew people side face because they don't know how else to draw them. But when you say they are lovely, it is not surprising; because primitive art is lovely too, isn't it?

You have overwhelmed me with the news that you intend to knit a second pull-over for me. But have you the time, Jill darling? I shouldn't consider it so necessary really. But take a kiss for being so sweet. You may send me only the warmth of your love. That should suffice even for these grey *weathers. Yes it does come across in spite of the coldness of paper – thought it could do better with some other medium.*

Give my very best regards to your mother. She must be a wonderful person I think. I think she can be told I am fine generally – though I have a nasty cold right now, which makes me feel petty. I should disinfect myself after reading this letter – or if I was pre-warned, before.

Moscow is celebrating the 40th Anniversary of the October Revolution.

It is all gay, bright and full of people from all lands again. Well, it is nice to see so many people all at once on the roads and so many types of faces. We have 3 days holidays due to this. This was badly needed, because we were all really overworked. The result is that the moment my nerves got a chance to relax, I fell ill. My work has not yet finished. That is awful but I expect it will be by 12th Nov. So I plan to leave on 13th Nov if I am lucky enough to get a ticket for that day, which I doubt due to the presence of many honourable guests here. However, it is too late a deliverance for me to think of running up to you, howsoever much I want it.

I shall be in Poland up to the end of January. My address will be c/o

Pani Skuszanka, Teatr Ludowy, Nowa Huta, Krakow.

You did not write to me if you have really decided to go to Munich in December and for how long.

I am not in the least certain what I am going to do after finishing my work in Poland. I rather feel I should be going home now, so it is possible I do not accept this invitation from the Budapest theatre after all. In that case, I should be turning up in London in February. Will you be there then?

I don't know whether I wrote to you or left it to your imagination that I had a few affairs in the last one and a half year that I have been in the continent. One of them was of a deeper nature and continues in a different form. The girl knows about you though.

Sometimes I dream that you may suddenly turn up in India as a renowned artist in a few years. I wonder how we should be then. Can you imagine?

But I wish to see you in London first and now – as soon as possible.

Well, look after yourself Jill my dearest girl. I shall expect to hear from you in Krakow next. Much work awaits me there and of a nature that frightens me a bit. So I shall need your letters all the more.

With the best of love,
Your Habib

I would have found it just as difficult then to answer your question as to what I felt about this letter, where Habib mentions the affairs he has had during his travels, as I find it today. The truth is, I was never good at confronting emotional complications unless I really had to – and in his own way, nor was Habib. Therefore I hadn't prepared myself at all for this news, and didn't know how to handle it.

It is quite extraordinary that after more than fifty years there still remains a very clear impression of my dilemma, for I was pitched into uncharted territory by what was not so much a confession as a passing remark. There is so much else of interest in this particular letter but I remember finding it hard to take it all in, because this information refused to fit in with other thoughts and bits of news. It stood out effortlessly as requiring a response. And you too have jumped on to it at once.

I tried to imagine how someone who felt so close to me could have 'a few affairs', which even appeared to melt into each other, except the one that he mentions continued 'in a different form'. What form? And what had happened to the others, I wondered. Did they not continue at all? Perhaps, yes surely, travelling made all the difference, for if one was only passing through then lovers could safely be left behind. This was a shocking thought, for it could well apply to me! But it must be so, for if they were all in one place (they had become 'all' to me by this time, not just 'a few'), wouldn't they be making a fuss and wanting to continue, bumping into each other in the same village or town, and exchanging their version of events?

And more confusing, so oblique was his news that he could not even remember whether or not he had mentioned it before. Yet, what leg had I to stand on to be disturbed, when I had my devoted Robin trying always to be at my side at Dartington? I hadn't told Habib of this warmest of friendships, not knowing what effect it would have on him if I wrote about it, or how important I should make it sound. I asked myself why I should write about it anyway, for I imagined that he would not know what to do with such information, just as I did not know what to do with his. These confusing thoughts engaged me for some time after reading Habib's letter. I must have written to him about my discomfort, however, for he mentions it at a later date and attempts some reassurance!

But incidentally, Mukti, on a lighter subject, I am beginning to agree with you about the knitting. I really think it's getting too much and Habib's politeness on the subject indicates, most delicately, that he was starting to think so too!

Thankfully, the first wretched garment does get to its destination quite soon. The second I don't think ever got finished.

Pani Skuszanka Warsaw
Teatr Ludowy 1.12.57
Nowa Huta. Krakow Poland

Dearest Jill,
I am continually running away from snow and continually encountering it wherever I go. Moscow had its first snow this year on the last day I was there. As I was leaving Berlin day before yesterday after spending a week there, it began to snow for the first time there in the aerodrome. As I landed here, Warsaw was experiencing its first snow and real winter. But I can run away no more. I have finally put my foot into it. I go to Krakow on 3rd, where I am sure much more snow waits for me. An extra severe winter for Europe is predicted this year anyhow. And I am to be in Krakow for at least 2 months. It is already too cold for my taste – br.r.r.r.! I got some useful books and music from Berlin for my production, and time to think and do some valuable paper work. Now I am helping the Polish translator with my copy of the English translation.

I do not know my programme in February after this work – quite as yet. But I think in about a fortnight – on receiving reply to my letter from Delhi – I shall know better. It seems Delhi needs me immediately, in which case I come to London in February. Will you then be there? I mean somewhere in the island?

This is a hurried extra note. But read love all along between the lines.

*Heaps of it. Many kisses,
Your Habib*

I am trying to imagine what Poland must have been like just twelve years after the war. Of course, it was a country that suffered horribly during that time, perhaps more than anywhere else in Europe, being the first country that was overrun by the Nazis. I'm sure it would have looked and felt pretty drab still. These conditions, plus the tough winter ahead, must have been daunting, but also perhaps there was a premonition that plans would not run smoothly in that country.

*Teatre Ludova Nowa Huta,
Krakow Poland
8.12.57*

*My dearest Jill
How lovely! That your letter should be waiting for me when I came here on the 3rd. And a nice long letter too – with so many interesting ideas – thoughts of the innermost recesses of your soul. I am inclined to agree with your religious ideas and with the idea that it is all so useless to bother about the*

mystery that may be God – though no doubt the 'Sputnik' is out to unveil it all over and forever in due course – soon enough maybe.

You seem to be influenced a little by the Hindu theory of the metempsychosis or the rebirth and re-incarnation of soul. A great Indian poet of the 19th Century (who wrote in Urdu) has a poem, which opens thus:

'Not all but a few became manifest in lilies and roses.

What wonderful beauties there might have been, (which are) now veiled in Earth!'

It's an imaginative and perhaps at the same time a most realistic account of the changing and changeable forms of matter at which you yourself have hinted in a different way. But then again I believe, optimistic-fashion, that one day Science will discover the mystery of life and death and perhaps be able to create life in laboratories and give longevity to some aristocrats – moneyed duds – and prove Shaw's biological theory (borrowed from a 19th Century French biologist) true – expounded in his 'Back to Methuselah'.

I have no programme for 'Xmas and can only expect a dull one.

Germany boasts of having the best 'Xmas in the world and in some respects, they are justified. But I am neither there nor in England where I speak the language nor in India. It will also be the time when I shall be most busy here. But perhaps I shall make some interesting friends by then. I shall write to you what happens – though I am resigned like a monk to my fate. What are you going to do. Aren't you going to Munich?

I am a little annoyed because my translator has not yet submitted the Polish text of the play, though he has been clamouring for me to come here for the past 6 weeks. Well, he is to send the text in a few days if you please, when it will be edited by me, from my English text and copied for artists – a fair 2 weeks work, which bring me on the verge of 'Xmas holidays of 5 days for the theatre. That simply means my actual rehearsals cannot start before January and the premiere before March – a glorious waste of time for me – seeing that the money I get is the same whether I stay one month or one year – and life is expensive here.

But I am ready with all my ideas and even a bit thrilled at the prospect.

Only if they can get translated in terms of theatre here!

I have been given a room to live in right here in the theatre building. It is a biggish, simple room, with a large bed and a large table – but warm enough. Well, for once I like it, I like the idea of living in a theatre – perhaps not for ever but for once it is thrilling. It is a feeling similar to that which Jean Louis Barrault had in his young days, when he was looking for work in the Comedie Francaise and stealthily spent one night in the miser's bed on stage. (I have forgotten the name of this promiscuous miser from Ben Johnson's play of the same name.)

Krakow as I had written to you is a beautiful old town. It was white with snow when I arrived here. It went on snowing for a couple of days, then turned into rain dirtying all the streets, then into clear sunny heart-warming weather, colder but more pleasant and cleaner; and now it again rains and makes everything miserable.

I have bought from Moscow a rather nice though expensive, camera. I have taken some nice photos with it, including some of my own self. Tomorrow I get the prints. So I might send one for you. Camera is a wonderful thing for Krakow, indeed for all travel and I am having lots of fun with it.

How did your concert come off? And how are your horn lessons now.

That song about a million deaths sounds terribly funny.

I know what you mean about the pain of breaking any kind of ties. It is a miniature form of death, isn't it? Shaw puts it in very much the same way when he says; 'Parting is one of the faces of death.' But I suddenly thought of Shaw after writing the great thought and felt flattered by such worthy corroboration.

Well, enough words. Yes, I am sure it will be terribly exciting meeting you once more after all this. I hope it is sooner than it looks. Meanwhile, all my love.

Habib

(ps)
I have written a new prologue for this Indian classic and I am going to do the small role of Stage Manager in the Polish language if you please. I might send you the text of this but in English some time. It is rather interesting I think.

Did I ever tell you that had I stayed to complete my Bristol term, I would have spent 6 weeks in Dartington Centre in a production there. Is it is as nice as it is made out?

I love this letter for its vividness and the care taken over the references, descriptions of living in the theatre with its atmosphere and excitement, the changing scenes of Krakow in winter. Also of course, the attention paid to my earnest 'soul' writings. It was a time in my life when, suffused with the influence of Dartington, the thinking of Tagore and the rich creative atmosphere, I was searching for profound meanings. That I could be taken seriously by someone as thoughtful as Habib was hugely gratifying and also encouraging.

Right now, however, it was my turn to express myself obliquely, for I was at the point of breaking up with Robin, about which I must have written something at least, for that would explain Habib mentioning the pain of parting. Our attachment was fading and losing its energy, and slowly coming to an end in a grievous and inexplicable way. Sadly, it was not so for both of us – it was me who was moving away and Robin who suffered the pain that goes with rejection. And there were no faults in him at all.

If you have not experienced such desperate pangs already, you almost surely will in the future. Few people living their lives to the full escape them. I remember learning a lot about how a young man can feel under such circumstances from Harry, a student who came to live in my house some years later. He was most unusual in that he could eloquently describe his deepest feelings, even the most painful, without self-pity. I got to know him very well over three years; he'd come upstairs quite often to eat with the family, and we had some marvellously interesting conversations about our lives. One evening, he told me that he'd had two affairs in his life and had resolved not to have any more until he found the right girl to marry. Of course I asked him why. He explained that the first girlfriend had dumped him all of a sudden and caused him deep shock and anguish, and he'd spent ages trying to get over her; the second he had dumped and that was equally terrible, resulting in a heavy sense of guilt and emptiness, again for a long time. I saw his point. Looking back, it can still make me feel uncomfortable that I should have caused an innocent person like Robin such unhappiness, especially as he was truly affectionate and loyal and wanted to take care of me. These early experiences do not get forgotten. I know the saying goes 'All's fair in love and war', but it doesn't help when you're in the middle of emotional turmoil. In fact, it's rather a silly phrase that trips off the tongue without saying anything in the least worthwhile.

You probably won't agree with my further thoughts on this subject, but here they are anyway: I have a notion that as individuals we humans share ourselves with each other much more subtly and more deeply than we may realize, especially when we are close. We borrow each other's ways of thinking and absorb each other's intelligence, tensions and moods on a daily basis, and adapt to each other constantly. So with each person with whom we are interacting we are just a bit different. When we have lost a person with whom this mingling took place at a deep level and feel, 'I will never be the same again', this is literally true. We cannot be the same again, for the relationship has been a unique entity whose elements can't be repeated. Shaw's words as quoted by Habib are very apt when you think about them: 'Parting is one of the faces of death.'

I think attitudes to love affairs have changed nowadays, but then, if you were deeply involved with someone, you kept it pretty quiet, especially from your parents. For one thing, if you were sleeping with your beloved, contraceptives being fairly rudimentary, there was always a fear of pregnancy that would bring shame and huge practical difficulties in its wake. For another, you tended to keep your very personal life out of sight of the rest of the family, for there was not the easy communication between its members that can exist now. There tended to be many more barriers between age groups – you did not expect to know much about your parents or their friends, and they probably felt the same about you.

In some ways, this absence of exposure could be experienced as rather a relief. It did mean there wasn't so much familiarity in the home and amongst relations, but with that sort of mild formality came a sense of privacy. I know, of course, that it also led to a lot of grief when children couldn't tell their parents what they were finding difficult to cope with in life. Getting the balance right in the home is difficult – and I guess it always will be.

Warsaw 12.1.58

Dearest Jill
Thanks a lot. What a lovely pull-over; it makes all the beautiful Polish girls of all the cafes look up at me. No, there is nothing wrong with the thing. It is just lovely. It could only have been made for me. And what a gorgeous blue. It seems to suit me so much that I myself am unable to take my eyes off me. But everyone says so. I walk with a certain air in it. And gosh it is warm. How shall I ever return so much love that is contained in every stitch of it Jill? How long did it take you to do it darling? It was

about to meet the same fate as your scarf in Hungary year before last. (Year before last! I have been away rather long, haven't I?) But it was redirected to me from Krakow only yesterday just in time. I wore it at once and have it on ever since.

Actually it forced me to write this letter to you. And of course all your beautiful letters too. And your very nice card.

The same reason which made me write all about snow to you kept me silent so long and still bids me silence but for your love. Well, I was waiting for something positive to write to you about. But now I am only waiting for something final. No, I am not producing the play. It is said by the translator that the text is not ready. Another translator is to be had. And he wouldn't be ready with it before March. So there! I have said it as briefly as possible.

But it is a long story which I will narrate to you some other time.

Just as my friends in India on seeing my new pull-over are bound to cry out what a wonderful country is England, I tend to generalise my present experience here too but try to fight very hard against this tendency.

I am not sure what I will do next. I am trying for many things. And next week I should be able to see my way more clearly perhaps, when I will certainly write to you at once. It is no use saying that one of the possibilities is to return to England and then India soon. One of the nastiest things is that I have not enough money even for replying to all the pending letters. But I am writing for newspapers and soon the situation would ease.

Both the weather and I were a bit gloomy when your

warm gift arrived bringing so much sunshine not only for me but the morose atmosphere of the Warsaw cafes as well. You were right about that splash of royal blue but wrong about the weather, which here in Poland at least attracts your attention during winter in a nasty way more than anything else. Girls? No, I must remain a monk for some more time. Your idea of me is not wrong Jill. I never really meant "many little affairs". What do you mean where did you pick up those British expressions? You have been teaching us English for 200 years Jill. Do send me that photo, Jill dearest. But write to my London address or wait until I can send my address.

Many, many, many warm kisses from Habib.

ps. I am thinking of returning to India by March or April in any case. I hope and I shall try that I can spend at least a month in England before that. In that case, I should see you pretty soon. I am so glad.

That was undoubtedly the best-timed present I ever sent! It is heart-warming that there is so much truly lyrical appreciation for the pullover in the teeth of such a big disappointment. And I was delighted that its bright blue had managed to brighten up the dreariness of post-war Poland.

For so long, I had tried hard to understand the difficulty that Habib would have on occasion with keeping in touch, putting it down to loss of interest or his being too busy. Not having the same problem, I would meanwhile concentrate as best I could on my singing and my friendships, but was always aware of a niggling sense of loss. This often resulted in a state of dreaminess as I tried to imagine my way into what could have happened. Eventually, I gained some insight into why he felt unable to express himself, which now seems pretty obvious but didn't at the time. I realized that keeping silent was often easier when he was worried or miserable about his life. But in turn, not communicating would accentuate his negative state of mind. He seemed to find a vast and satisfactory outlet in absorbing himself in his work, if work there was, and would wait for some outside pressure to make him open up again. There is that odd little phrase which stands out particularly: 'Actually it forced me to write this letter to you...' There were times when he was not able to get in touch with anyone, not even his mother when she badly needed to have news of him, and those times were nearly always during great difficulties and depressions, the Polish let-down being a minor example of what was to follow in later years.

This might be the right place to try to answer the question you were asking earlier: Which religion did Habib follow? In what did he have faith? Or perhaps the question should be: what kept him going in times of great stress? As far as his beliefs were concerned, I don't think he was an atheist, but he couldn't have taken up a traditional position regarding religion because he would almost surely have found the demands and restrictions involved too much to handle. You are not unlike Habib in this respect, Mukti, with your strong desire to be open-minded and original in your way of thinking, not to be fixed. I didn't ever observe or feel that he followed any particular religion or philosophy. Although he was born into quite a traditional Muslim family, with a father who expected much of him in that direction, he shook the influence off and took up his own path. As you know, he became a social activist who believed in the power of artists, and in particular of theatre, to bring about social change. Many of his plays were political, and as such got him into a good deal of trouble with the establishment, for which he had little respect. He truly loved working with his troupe of actors, handpicked very often from the lowest echelons of Indian society, and seeing him moving amongst them it was obvious that their humour, energy and talents fascinated and invigorated him. The bourgeoisie he detested and also any form of humbug – two pet hates upon which he elaborates later. In his interaction with his actors, both could be avoided in his day-to-day working life; it was a very good arrangement that lasted for over half a century.

B/ Magdefrau, Pestalozzistr.12 Stendal. G.D.R
28.2.58

Jill dearest,
On return to Berlin a couple of weeks ago, I got two splendid letters from you dated 5 Nov. 57 and 5 Feb. 58. The first is an angry letter all about the jersey and a demand for a photo from me, which I enjoyed reading much more. Because I quite love your cross moods specially in letters. And this was wonderfully written. You have got a snap from me since; but I am sending you another just in appreciation of your sweet demand. This is taken by myself with my own camera kept static in my room in Krakow in the last rays of the setting sun; and the shadows have come out rather nice I think, don't you?

The photo Habib took in Krakow

I should love to see your clay model when I come. I guess it must be cute. But more than that I am dying to hear you sing. You will sing for me, Jill darling, won't you? You were so mean about it in the past.

I love your new photo. It's adorable. Thanks a lot for that. You certainly have changed and grown, Jill. You look more cute still. It would be wonderful to see you again after nearly 2 years, when I get back in April.

Yes, that's when I plan to be in London. I shall fly from Berlin by the end of March and spend about a week or ten days in Dusseldorf and Brussels before I come to you. I have some nasty new problems here.

They concern my excess baggage. I am going to leave a lot of it behind; but even then it is much. It can only go by air and that costs a lot of money. In my case it is going to be more difficult still because I have no west marks and one must only pay in west marks. I am not earning west *marks either. So, to tell you quite simply, it would mean for me four times the actual costs. That's nasty. So I have taken up lodgings in a small town near Berlin for cheap living and started earning in right earnest. I came here recently. While in Berlin, I was awfully busy. So that accounts for my silence. You can write to me on above address upto 20th March or you can use my Berlin address.*

The latter should do till the end of March.

I hope to be able to spend at least a month in England, though I don't know how I would do it. I have only 2 pounds in my bank there. I expected about 200 coming from my Indian scholarship but now I don't know when I should get it, if at all. So I must think of some very paying jobs if I want to send my 16 packages home and also stay for some time to look up my friends and get used to their changed faces.

There was spring-like weather here too till a couple of weeks ago, but it is now reversed to snow, fog, rain and sunshine. In a way I am glad because it gives me more chance to show off my beautiful jersey, and I hope for the sake of your new fur shoes you are again having the usual nasty English winter.

Stendal is a little place but old and nice and cheap. It is near Tangamunde, a smaller place, Germany's first capital. I went there last Sunday and found wonderful material for my camera. On my return I shall have hundreds of photos to show you. But where are you likely to be in April? I hope not out of England. Did you go out anywhere in the recent past or do you plan to, next Spring?

Thanks ever so much for those beautiful words asking me to look after myself during these travelings, Jill dear.

They had a touching ring – coming as they did after what happened in Poland. I am just about tired of traveling and now long to stay in one place without work and no worry about petty extraordinary problems.

Don't be angry again Jill for my long silence. I have been framing words for all my thoughts for you nearly every day for a long time but never got the time to put them on paper. When I got it I only managed to write the dull letter that this is. But I send you the warmest kisses – provided of course there is room for them in your 'Farm' full of ducks and dogs and cats and what not. Love,

Yours Habib.

I don't remember at what point I first sang for Habib, but I certainly feel guilty that it didn't happen more often. It was not that easy to do so in actual fact, because the sort of singing I was involved in needed accompaniment of a piano or an organ, which were not always available. By this time I was singing a lot of 'Lieder', which consists of German songs by composers such as Schubert and Schumann, and great works of oratorio which need a concert hall or a church for their performance. My voice had settled down into a 'classical English contralto' and I was undergoing training at Dartington as a classical singer with a very stiff and conventional singing teacher. The result was that I experienced singing as much more difficult than it should have been. So rigid was my teacher that it took me years of trying to relax to get over his training.

Much later in my life it occurred to me that your mum's way of singing, with a guitar or harp as accompaniment, was much more fun, and ultimately more moving to listen to. There have been so many lovely occasions when she has sung just off the cuff at home for the pleasure of it, accompanying herself with one or the other, and I have sung along with her, feeling much more comfortable than up on a stage. Habib enjoyed many such occasions and eventually brought Nageen along to our two houses in France (which was when you and I met them, and you wheeled him around Heathrow Airport, if you remember), where she could experience singing together with us. I know that one of his greatest wishes was to have his two daughters – Anna and Nageen – singing together in public, but sadly no such opportunity presented itself during his lifetime. 'My two pearls' was how he referred to his daughters as he pottered about the French kitchen half a century after his great European tour, at the age of eighty-four. I particularly like the way your mum has managed to bridge both worlds of classical and folk singing and she carries her accompanying instruments with her, and I did envy Habib his ability to just sing wherever he happened to be; my style of singing felt out of place in someone's sitting room or under a tree. Since then I have often thought how wonderful it is to sing as a free expression and do it just when you feel like it, but it has taken me a long, long time to get to that point of happy informality.

At the time of this last letter Habib would have been travelling for well over two years, earning his way from country to country. You know, Mukti, I am struck with the thought yet again – that it was a remarkable achievement. Each country would have presented different problems, if not of climate, then of communication and contacts, not to mention accommodation, finding your way around and finding friends. No wonder he expresses a sense of weariness and a strong need to be settled somewhere or other.

I need to stand back for a moment and tell you briefly what it is about this correspondence that makes it so very personal and extraordinary for me. I feel you might have wondered why I have been so moved by these letters. Yes, I know they are addressed to me and that he was hugely important in my life, but even so, there's something else to add. Some of them are certainly less interesting than others, being repetitive and full of apologies for late answers, but even so I can't help but be aware of the particular rhythm of the words and their inflections – it's not just their content that strikes me. Through them, I can hear Habib's voice and his pauses for breath, just as if he were saying these things directly into my ear; they really are full of life. Whatever is meant by death seems to be momentarily defied; it's just as if his own unique expressiveness is still pulsing away. I'm not sure that anyone else reading them who hadn't known him would feel this, but I'm sure those who did would recognize these strong and particular resonances. They are what I hear most clearly, and I stop still and feel his presence.

Stendal 17.3.58

My dearest Jill,
Got your beautiful letter of 10 March on my arrival back from Berlin today 15th March. But the date above should be right because tomorrow being Sunday and I have no stamps, this letter can't get posted until Monday.

I have a cold and feel rather down in the mouth; so the extra warmth in your letter was so badly needed and welcome.

I should love it. To come to Sanduck I mean. I think it is wonderful investment of my money. I should have to make a brief halt in London though to explore my prospects a bit. I didn't quite get you when you said you might see me in London. Shall we go together? Is that the idea? Why do you say it would be easier to see me in London than in Sanduck Farm? If I get you right, that's a bit disconcerting, isn't it? But I am sure I am wrong.

The money problem should ease up a great deal, should Moscow get it into its head to pay me (in pounds in London) in time for my write-ups about Indian theatre; which they are going to do in any case though in their own sweet time. I feel a bit hectic because I am due back home by April end.

The theatre in Delhi needs me for producing 'Chalk Circle'.

You are quite right about that photo; but you can't expect a smile Jill dear, if you adjust a camera on time and the automatic switch yourself and then run to your place to be snapped – all in 14 seconds' time. I only like its shadows. You should try my camera when I come if you want a smile.

You may be quite right about that book being a vast lie. It's a long story which needs time to tell. It was not one but several books, or at least several chapters of several books, none of which got published. I was only running into the funniest publishers who demanded samples of chapters, liked them, promised to undertake contracts, considered and parleyed for money, and after getting me to write much stuff said they could bring out that chapter in their paper as an article but the authorities forbid that subject for a book for our publishing house just yet. These books then become articles on Indian Music, dance, literature etc. I was not sorry because I got some money anyhow; but the worst of all such things was a story, which at first threatened to turn from a novel-let into a novel and then got reduced from a novel-let into a short story, all because of the whims of publishers and my stupid tenacity.

I tried to sell it in all forms but failed. Failed after nearly succeeding apparently every time. But since I have still not ceased to try, I have no right to tell you of its biography. This story – and if you care, all the wretched articles – you can certainly have the pleasure of reading when I come. What is it about? Love of course. Set in a village of Western India. Full of songs, colour, spectacle! The plot I cannot tell you because then I have to write the story for you all over again. But I think one might say it is a tragedy. It has no happy end anyhow.

Now, all that off my chest, how about a song sung in the Sanduck Farm setting!

If you knew what petty problems are keeping me here you would be both surprised and vastly amused. But if I were to write all that down, you would hate me for the long and tiresome letter. If I had my way, I would fly tomorrow. But can't do it before the end of March. I shall write to you when I come.

I think it was lovely of your mother to say it would be fine if I came.

You have no idea how glad I am. Wary? Perhaps a little. Perhaps. But I always wanted to see the place and you in your own setting. And I am going to make it even if I have just time to say hello and goodbye and then catch my plane and even if the fare is 2 pounds one pence.

Give my love to your fat Lin-Yutang-white-S. African, if any is saved from you. God bless you for that lovely letter. Kisses.

Yours, Habib

PS If you see that you are likely to reach me here before the end of March and want it, write to the following address:-
Berlin – Zehlendorf, Quermatenweg 148, b/Schroder
 It is ridiculous I have forgotten the address of Dartington Art Centre and can't think of its being longer than that. But that must be wrong; so I send this to Sanduck. Hope you get it soon enough.

Did my courage momentarily fail me when I imagined bringing Habib to Sanduck Farm? Yes, I have to admit with a considerable sense of misgiving, that it did. I was frightened that his welcome would not be of the warmest and that I would have to watch his feelings being hurt. This was an agonizing thought after so much eager anticipation of the event. I must have conveyed some hesitation to which he has responded sensitively. Remembering this opens up a whole vista of those times, when bringing a boyfriend back to meet your parents could be hazardous, let alone if he also happened to be a foreigner, and coloured to boot! If he took it into his head to disapprove of someone, my father could be visibly unfriendly. Habib picked up on my uncertainty immediately – I feel sad even now to think he had to face this – but, fortunately, he seemed to rally with the encouraging thought that my mother would be warm and accepting.

It is difficult to imagine today that such issues really could cause hours of lost sleep, but I did have some experience of them – being barged into and elbowed off pavements by large people in London who noticed my arm was linked with Habib's as we went shopping together, later being turned away from little hotels (which evidently had vacancies), because of his colour – this was quite normal in the '50s, when it was quite permissible for landlords to put up notices outside their houses reading NO BLACKS NO IRISH NO DOGS.

By the '60s, I think things were loosening up a little, at least among the young, and for this we might look to the influence of the Beatles and their connections with Indian gurus, which undoubtedly opened up new, if confusing, aspects of the East. Musically as well, there was a mingling of influences thanks to the interactions between them and Ravi Shankar, and all this filtered through slowly to mitigate the fear that goes with racism.

I don't think the older generation was much changed. The hippie movement evolved and was for them another cause for fear – all that 'free love' along with drugs, along with not earning, and what on earth was 'Flower Power' anyway? So, amongst most older people in England, wariness was still uppermost concerning this 'New Age'. Today we are supposed to be a tolerant multi-cultural society but I don't believe that this is quite the case.

That I could have wished the photo with the dark shadows to be any different is hard to understand, because now it is one of my favourite snaps. I think it was mainly that Habib looked a lot thinner in the face by this time, which gave me a shock. All the same, reading such a reaction makes me cross with myself for the stupid rigidity of taste it shows. The 'fat Lin-Yutang' reference is tucked well into the recesses of my mind and refuses to surface, as does the long reference to the book project he was involved with. Possibly this endeavour got thrown out with many other papers due to excess baggage problems. It's rather a forlorn thought that my own letters probably met with the same fate!

Stendal 17.3.58

My dearest Jill,
Got your delightful letter of 30th March. Good. Jolly good. I love the idea of travelling with you in a train to your home. I am expecting to be in London round about 20 April. I shall send you a telegram. I should just like to spend about 3 or 4 days in London in order to send away all my luggage lying with my agents. It is enormous work, because it involves about 16 huge and immovable packages and that would mean some packing and unpacking. After this however, I am quite free. It would suit me fine to be with you in London during this time, if you would not hate me to be so busy with petty things. Anyway, evenings I would certainly compensate for my hectic days. Do, do try that and if possible, come to London for the whole of this time. I am flying to Bruxelles in 2 or 3 days; then after spending 2 or 3 days in Bruxelles to London. I am due in Delhi by the end of the month. I hate it. So far they

left me so free. And now suddenly, they have pulled the rope. It is really awful.

I am so very, very glad to be able to see you again soon and be with you but at the same time very unhappy that I can't stay as long as I had wished. But even then I want to stretch it as long as possible.

All my love and all my kisses,

Yours Habib

The timing of these plans sounded alarmingly tight, leaving just a very few days when Habib would be present but busy. The farm visit, so much discussed and looked forward to, would be a matter of two or three days perhaps. If he really had to be in Delhi by the end of the month, how would it all fit in and give us time to get used to each other after such a long separation? Although I longed deeply for us to be together, I was apprehensive about the terrific sense of rush, of trying to fit everything in. I am a slow person when it comes to adapting – not good at sudden changes and sudden moves – and found it difficult to understand why there was so little time, yet again, for us to savour.

Habib was restless and always on the move, yet capable of intense concentration that he could sustain for many hours, even throughout the night, when working. And although the idea of staying put in a homely context seemed to appeal to him once work was finished – and he often said how much he longed for time off – he very seldom availed himself of such opportunities. I don't believe he ever planned any visit anywhere for more than a few days if there was not the possibility of becoming involved in a creative project – rehearsing or seeing plays, or performing one thing or another. And this tendency to keep moving became more pronounced as time went by and his life became more complicated, so eventually it became difficult to keep track of arrangements. Which one would work out? Would he be very late? Would he turn up at all? And yet his timing in dramatic terms was incredibly good and he was well known for it. Perhaps to have mastery of both sorts of timing is rare – that of life and of theatre. Perhaps, in the very nature of things, one even cancels the other out? I don't know what the answer is to that question, but I never did quite manage to catch on or catch up.

Berlin 19.4.58

Dearest Jill,
I was ill. I am better now. Just cold accompanied by some nasty things.
To spare you the shock, I have lost about 28 pounds in the last 2 years in Europe. In England, I had gained. I am hanged if I know from where possibly I could lose any weight. If I have really gained experience abroad as people say, it must be a very poor show in weight.
Here's a photo with a grin, which you wanted. But I come soon. And then you can see me like a Cheshire Cat, smiling from ear to ear on seeing you.
I am thrilled.
Love,

Yours in a hurry,
Habib

And so he did arrive, yes, grinning like a Cheshire Cat, a very slender one. And I too grinned and cried, and overwhelmingly felt the joy and surprise of this return – the wonder of it. I took days off from Dartington for which I had to beg, and met him in London at Waterloo station. It was very strange and arresting, hugging such a fragile frame. We made that journey by train together to Devon, at last – such a long awaited journey. My brother was at the farm as was my father. My mother made everything very smooth with her warm welcome and to my great relief there was no awkwardness with my father. He liked Habib. My brother Kev was eager for intense discussions on matters that concerned him – which incidentally are similar to your concerns, Mukti. He was trying to sort out the significance of his own life on so many different levels at the age of twenty-one – and this was very fitting because some real exchanges took place in which Habib contributed with equal intensity.

We walked the dogs and visited some sheep, ate well and even managed to call on some unusual neighbours a couple of miles away who asked us to stay for dinner – John and Audrey Keir-Cross. John was writing the script for *The Archers* (a hugely popular farming saga that is still broadcast on BBC Radio 4) and so was able to let us in on the latest stories that were soon to unfold. Audrey, now nearly ninety, remembers that dinner. It was May, probably the most beautiful month of the year, and all was tender and relaxed. But very short.

The pressing need was to get away further, for a few more days, and to have an adventure just on our own. The difficulty was getting those extra days off and away from my college. Having deposited Habib on a train back to London, I returned to Dartington and ruminated on how to do this: where should I say I needed to go and why? It would involve going to see the principal to ask for his permission. What story could I make up that would cover my absence? I couldn't say I wanted to go away with the man I loved, truly to be together with him at long last, could I? It was the truth, but I couldn't see how I should word such a request. It seemed to me that even in the liberal climate of Dartington, it would not go down well.

But after much thought, that is in fact what I did. Most surprisingly, the frank interview that ensued turned out to be one of the most sincere and rewarding encounters I can remember. I do believe that the romance in which I was involved, and the fervour with which I conveyed its importance, was infectious. What else could have influenced such an unlikely outcome? Our principal, Richard Hall, normally quite an austere person and no longer young, hesitated, then visibly warmed. My honesty was rewarded, permission was given and even came with a blessing. And so Habib and I took off for Bristol, familiar to him but a place I had missed visiting three years earlier.

We wandered around Bristol, at last able to turn to each other fully but not able to find a hotel that would accept us. Meanwhile, very ordinary activities like sipping tea in a cafe and chatting about travels, songs and books took on a magical aura suffused with untold meaning. We must have looked a rather odd couple – this very thin Indian man, poorly dressed but remarkably handsome and even somehow elegant, together with a much younger girl, both enveloped in a complete haze of romance. At last, on the third attempt to find somewhere to stay, a landlady took pity on us even though it must have been obvious that we were not married. I remember clearly that first of all she hesitated and muttered, indicating that there were no vacancies. Then, on seeing our crestfallen expressions she melted, suddenly finding that indeed there was one room for us after all – it was a wonderful breakthrough. So we made our warm and luxurious nest for a matter of just a few nights, with her blessing. This was fortunate indeed, for at that time you had at least try to look married, and sign the hotel visitors' book as if you were, or there would be little hope of finding somewhere to sleep. And if you were a mixed race couple you would almost certainly be frowned upon whatever the status of your relationship.

London 12.5.58

Jill my darling girl,
Kisses for that lovely letter.
Even in order to feel feelings and think thoughts, one needs time and more time to be able to express them in words. Time and Peace of mind. I envy you.

I wanted to go last Saturday. Failed. Tried Sunday. Failed again. Booked for Tuesday. Could not get Czech visa. They said they want 2 weeks even in order to give a 2 hour visa. Then booked Wednesday. But money was becoming a more irksome problem. Got a talk assignment at the British Drama League for Wednesday. So now the first plane after Wednesday is Monday 19th May via Dusseldorf to Berlin. Yes, now I am taking this route, because this involves no visas.

I have spent a hectic time and I am very tired. The only time I got to think and feel deeply and to my full satisfaction was the time I spent in the train from Bristol. It was like fragrance – you were the flower.

I am glad about your letter – very glad. Wanted to write to you, when I knew my programme. I came to know it only today. Can never write a letter like you wrote.

Can you not make a supreme effort and spend the next week-end in London? But only if you can do it without causing much disturbance around you.

I got the parcel at last. Your letter was sweet. Give heaps of thanks from me to your Dad for the fiver. I can't return it in the near future. But though it came late, it was a great help. I hope to be able to acknowledge the debt more gratefully some time.

Best regards and thanks to your mother too for the trouble and to John and Audrey. Love to their kids. I shall try to contact Kevin some time.

All my love to you Jill, my sweet.

Habib

PS I think it would be alright at Aaley's House, if you decide to come. I could ring you up if you give me a time. Or you could ring me up Shepherd Bush 6217 in the morning up to 9.30. It would be better though if you told me the time first.

A kiss
Yours Habib.

The handwriting shows what a rush Habib was in. It's written on the run, but very precious nonetheless for confirming that he had been happy being with me, just as I had been with him.

I could not get up to London that following weekend as I had musical commitments at Dartington and I did not dare stretch my concession to take further days off. So far nobody had got fed up with me (except for Robin, who looked on in sad amazement at my behaviour, the results of which put me into a state of impenetrable dreaminess for weeks to come), but they soon would, if I were to disappear again.

How tiny our spell together was – just a few days. I can hardly believe that so much could come together in such a short time, after such a very long wait, but it left me with a strong sense of incompleteness, of being in limbo, which was like an ache. Something so big which felt so inevitable was unfolding – now where was it to go?

Dusseldorf 19.5.58

My dearest Jill,
When it came to telephoning you on Sunday evening, I realised that I had lost your number. Cursed be this forgetfulness, I have lost in London to date, a gold ring, an expensive pipe and a valuable telephone number. I hope I don't discover more losses.

I was exasperated by London – packing, unpacking, and re-packing, running around in tubes, worrying continually for money. It was only during the last 3 days that I managed to earn quite enough by a talk at the B.D.L., a programme in 'In Town Tonight' and 2 other BBC talks. Got more than £20 for all this. The irony of it, however, is that this morning, an hour before my coach was to leave for the aerodrome, I got a letter from the Govt. of India saying that they have decided in my favour – that means they would let me have my scholarship money for one more year i.e., till May 59. It was too late either to get or make any immediate use of this money, which must be a hell of a lot.

Please don't forget to let me have your father's initials and his bank address.

I am writing to you from the aerodrome. I fly to Berlin in half an hour.

After 3 days, I go to Prague (c/o Drahotov, Cinska 10 Prague – Dejvice) which I leave on 27th May for Zurich, c/o DUBS, which I leave n 29th May for Rome, which I leave on 31 May for New Delhi (c/o Grindlays Bank, CONNAUGHT CIRCUS, New Delhi – for the time being as long as I am homeless). I shall get to Delhi on the evening of first June, unless I quickly and unexpectedly succeed in getting the Pakistan visa enabling me to spend 2 or 3 days instead of 2 hours in Karachi, where I have hosts of relatives and friends.

I am very, very tired Jill darling. Every limb aches. I had managed to catch a silly cold in London. Soon it should all be over though.

It is nice and warm and the flight was good. It was a super-constellation. Air India have jolly good service now. At the moment I am in air, flying BEA, another beautiful flight.

Well, you couldn't come, love. I understand, though I missed you intensely. 'Missed' is not it. I yearned for you. If these stupid people in India House, who had been corresponding with me for 2 years only remembered my *address and instead of sending their letter to Bristol sent it on to my correct address, I would have got it as early as 15th May and then with a fat bank balance like that – must be in the neighbourhood of £200 – couldn't I again run up to you to South Brent for the weekend again, if of course you could conveniently join me. Can't get over the misery of not being able even to talk to you on phone. The only solace is that I am now still more sure of returning, because at least I am quite sure of the return fare now.*

Who were the unfortunate people courting death, Jill? Boy and girl in love or what? And why? What a disaster! Do let me know more of this. It is tragic.

You should have been a saint. I think you are. Anyhow, you are an angel. I envy you enormously for your peace – your clear form of happiness – I would give anything to learn it from you.

Saw a terrible show, 'Henry VIII' at the Old Vic and a nice one of 'My Fair Lady'.

You should have listened to my songs on 'In Town Tonight'. They were not badly received at all.

Do write to me about your health by the end of the month, won't you, love?

Don't lose your secret of good cheer. Kisses all over you,

Yours, Habib

So many near misses! Small ones, like not knowing about the *In Town Tonight* programme which would have been so exciting to listen to, and then huge ones, like the scholarship money just not arriving in time.

That I could come across as having such a clear sense of happiness is really extraordinary under such circumstances. I wonder how I managed it? Perhaps it was the rare joy of catching up with Habib, at last, that created that impression. Yes, I'm sure that was the case. The rest of the time I certainly spent wondering about the future, and when and how meetings could be managed. Often, there seemed to be no solution.

The tragic story of two young people to which he makes intriguing references simply escapes my memory. I must have written in the vaguest terms about it at the time and today I cannot dredge up the details.

Berlin
27.5.58

My dearest Jill,
Just a hurried note to tell you that I still find myself waiting for the Prague visa. This has incidentally also involved cancellation of all my previous bookings for the journey home. It seems to me now that the earliest I can leave Berlin for Prague is 30th, if I get the visa tomorrow. Anyhow, Prague should find me there right upto 2nd June at least. Now I don't know whether I would break journey at Zurich and Rome at all. If you can get me in Prague, do write at once. I feel strange, being cut off from you so completely. You would be hearing from me again. I am absolutely miserable and full of self-pity. It is today's weather I suppose, which makes one feel so cold and lonesome. With all my love and heaps of kisses,

Your
Habib

I too felt completely cut off and lonesome thinking of Habib on his way back to India – and rushing through so many different places on the way; why, I wondered? – and was already thinking how I could reach him. Dartington seemed to have detached itself from the central meaning of my life and I could not get back to my old involvements there, nor was it time to move on.

Letters had suddenly become very inadequate.

5

Raipur 28.6.58

Jill
Why are you silent darling?
   I don't remember to have been in a worse state of depression ever before. Your silence does not improve this.

It is hard to re-adjust quickly. With time, I hope it can be done. I feel terribly alone and isolated. I see stupidity, ignorance, poverty, dirt, egotism & dirt around me. As yet there seems no one, who thinks alike, with whom one could talk and be happy a little, and whom one could call a friend. I dream about past and I dream about the future, but there is nothing in the present to engage one's attention. I dream of my life abroad in the past and of the same in the future. It is a silly state, which I do not like. I want to shake it off. I get a sudden feeling sometimes that I don't want to do any work at all.

Occasionally I get the stupid idea of coming to England and living – just living – earning enough to live – that's all – and goodbye to all dreams – or go to America – or anywhere else. I think on my return to Delhi I shall get myself medically examined thoroughly. Maybe some sickness in my body is producing this sickness of the mind. No, but seriously.

I hope work in Delhi does it – rehabilitates me. Will it?

For love, I am in a desert. Not a drop of water, not a patch of green. Not even a mirage in these disillusioning sands. Hard, disobliging realities stand out like rocks, glistening against a sun, which produces 116 to 120 degrees of heat. And this seems an endless stretch. Not even a fellow traveller in sight. Not even any sound of their wailings. Not even your own echo. Not even a sense of movement, nor any urge for it. It is a peerless state in its perfection.

I know it is all so much nonsense. But must tell someone all the stupid things going on in the heart. To you I wanted to say more cheerful things.

But sorry I can't. There is no one else, of whom I could be sure that would hear all this with any kind of understanding. Perhaps all this would change in a week or 2 weeks. Perhaps not. I don't know. Can you help? How?

Well, just write. Just write all about yourself. That might be enough. Many things that haunt the mind – the Bristol days of Spring for instance – they might re-provide a source of joy, at least a sense of reality of some significance, some meaning. How are you, my own Jill? How are you? Why must you be so utterly silent, when I must be thirsting to hear from you.

Lots and lots and lots of warmest love and kisses, from

Your Habib.

I remember well getting this letter, for of course it shocked me with its distressing messages. You ask me, Mukti, why I was silent when I'd been such a terrific letter writer when Habib was in Europe? I think it all seemed to me quite useless by this time, writing endless letters when the other person was actually present for such a brief time. Even so, I couldn't sleep for thinking about how difficult Habib's life was and how lonely, and how badly I wanted to join him. I was still at Dartington but soon to leave for Germany, where I didn't want to go. One night, shortly after hearing from him, when I was home for the weekend at the farm and feeling particularly desperate, I got up from my bed and went to my mother's room. She was still awake, reading. I simply stood there in front of her at the end of her bed and said, 'I have to go to India. I know I must.'

She was terrified, and didn't hide her fears. 'You can't go at your age, all by yourself!' she exclaimed. 'We won't allow it.'

This was the first time she had used 'we' when it came to family decisions, meaning my father and her. It sounded very strange and false because my father was not normally in the least bit interested in what we, as grown-up offspring, did. Nor did she normally consult him. I supposed it showed the extent of her discomfort. She was adamant, and I knew very well I didn't have the money to set off without some parental cooperation, nor, when it came down to it, the courage to make such a huge journey unsupported.

I have wondered since if she was so frightened for me because at the age of twenty, only a year older than I was, she had set off for Australia to marry my father – and had met with very considerable difficulties. A man less unsuited to family life would have been hard to find. Perhaps she saw me following in her footsteps, pursuing a relationship that was neither substantial nor reliable. Who knows exactly what my mother was thinking, but she kept up her objections quite persistently, and eventually undid my immediate resolve.

So Germany and Munich it was to be but, as it transpired, not for long. From the moment I set off in that direction I felt I was making a mistake. The country grated on me: the harsh language; the relentless hard work and efficiency of the Germans; my singing teacher who was small and fierce like a terrier whilst I was tall and slow and rigid when it came to singing for her; my family residence where I was one girl too many in a family of five sisters and one brother. It all felt pointless and alien.

Month after month I waited for news of Habib. And I wondered what on earth I was doing in Germany, increasingly aware that I shouldn't be there but not yet sure how to get out of it.

> *c/o The Hindustani Theatre, House No. 22*
> *Low cost Housing Exhibition, Mathura Road,*
> *New Delhi 9.8.58*

> *Dearest Jill,*
> *I am sorry for keeping silent for so long. You have no idea how busy I was and in what a mess I am. Got 2 wires from my mother because I could not bring myself to write to her all this time. My luggage is lying at the docks in Bombay for nearly 2 months and since I did not even bother to contact my agents, I have to pay heavy demurrage charges. So I have sold my new German typewriter even before I could use it.*
>   *It is not so much production, with which I am busy, but re-organization of a theatre which is badly organized, to say the least. It is just work, work, work – all alone – and a lot of headache – and the prospects are dubious yet.*
>   *I am still looking for a house and a cook – life is unsettled – food in restaurants is bad and expensive – I am sharing life with another writer, his house and kitchen – for the time being.*
>   *My sterling is still lying at the India House London and they have threatened to make the payment to me here in rupees. I don't want this. So I have to argue and fight with the cultural ministry here and eventually if they agree,*

give them Power of Attorney to transfer my funds to my London bank.

It is only then that I would be able to return your father's fiver. I am so ashamed.

No, I just can't leave India for at least another 7 or 8 months, maybe more. If I succeed in building this theatre here in a very short time, which is a bit doubtful, I might be able to leave in April. Else I have to stick it out till I feel the theatre is strong enough to stand on its own legs.

Financially speaking, I am extremely poor. But that has never worried me, except an occasional feeling that it is high time I had a better life which funnily I feel I deserve.

But perhaps you would like to spend some holidays in India some time.

I could try to save some money for that. Then I must plan my life better.

And start doing some other jobs as well – like radio and journalism. I might arrange some lucrative concerts for you when you come. Oh go on, Jill, what else can I write darling. I miss you despite much work. The lips have forgotten what it is like to kiss a girl. But every fibre throbs with past sensations sometimes. And the heart aches. How are you my sweet?

Love Habib

When I received this letter, hardly more cheerful than the last, I had already come to this conclusion: staying in Germany was not going to work out for me. By this time I'd made a few friends outside of my 'family' and one of them suggested I move out and come to Austria – to Salzburg, in fact – where she had contacts who could find me a room. In fact, I remember quite vividly how I came across this particular friend. I had been sitting in a restaurant in the bohemian area of Munich ruminating on my life, slowly sipping my coffee and pondering, when I noticed that in the large gold-framed mirror hanging on the wall in front of me was reflected the solemn face of a girl who was gazing at me. Her hair was quite long and fine and framed her expression rather winningly. She looked a bit sad and thoughtful, rather like I was feeling, and all of a sudden she smiled at me, still in the mirror. I smiled back and she left her table and came around to mine. So we began to talk.

It turned out she was of Jewish extraction, born in Argentina, and had trained as a doctor before coming over to Germany. She was not happy with that occupation, however, and wanted to be a writer. Her theme was most unusual. She wanted to write a book championing the 'cause' of men and lampooning that of women. She felt strongly that women manipulated men to get their own way and were much the more fortunate sex. Since feminism was at that point burgeoning rapidly all over the Western world, this seemed to me a very courageous and somewhat risky project. Margareta, as she was called, felt it was important that the case for men's rights be made with a strong voice, even though she knew it would make her very unpopular with her own sex. Although I didn't entirely agree with her point of view, we became friends and she did eventually write *The Manipulated Man* under the name of Esther Vilar. She became very famous or, rather, infamous, and was pilloried for her writing, even receiving death threats.

Meanwhile, in the restaurant, I told her of my life, about coming to Germany when I was reluctant to do so, and that I was wondering how I could get out of my situation. She pointed out that Austria was a lot more relaxed than Germany – I'd like it better there and still be able to learn singing and German. She had friends in Salzburg who would no doubt put me up. Much though I disliked unsettling myself, this is the move I made, setting off into the unknown shortly after meeting Margareta, finding the room and making contact with a school of music (of which there were many, this being Mozart's birthplace) to continue studying singing. I remember thinking: 'This is the sort of moving about that Habib did for years all over Europe, so I should be able to do the same.' You needed luck with people and not worry about what would happen next, I told myself. I made myself adopt those attributes but, actually, only in a very small sense were they useful. The core that would have held the whole experience together was missing in my case, for I simply didn't want to be trekking around Europe. My heart was not in it, and loneliness and a sense of pointlessness set in once more. After three months I simply couldn't see what I was supposed to be doing there.

New Delhi 13.10.58

Gillette darling,
Sorry for silence. But often my sweetest thoughts have been with you.
   That is whenever time permits it. That happens mostly at bed time. But sometimes, memories come crowding into an overworked brain even in the middle of intense

activity. Yes, I am awfully busy and a bit lonesome. Not a single friend here either. But hardly time for friends. I hope my present experiment in theatre succeeds. It is a big experiment in music, dance and drama all at once, with a cast of 36 amateurs all untrained, and no one to assist me in a creative way. The show takes place on 1st December.

I envy you being in Munich. I wish I was there with you. But you might not regret being here either specially at this time. The weather is just superb. The air is so crisp you could dig your teeth into it. It is like the best European day in Summer – South Europe I mean. If you can really come now, what is the hitch? If you want to come in February, do that. It would be cold weather then and still lovely. Summer alone is horrid in Delhi, but that is just over and a long way off now.

Future plans I am quite unable to make at the moment. I am getting about £23 per month and a room with kitchen and bathroom to live in. I find it very hard to live on this amount. I do not find time to do other work and earn some more. But if this experiment comes off at all, I might get more money from the theatre and also more time to do other work. I am not yet sure, however, whether I would stick to this particular organization. The situation might become clearer for me in a couple of months time.

I plan also to visit Europe either in April or June '59. About this too I am not in a position to decide right now.

To add to all this confusion, my rehabilitation in my own country after a long absence is not yet complete. I keep remembering foreign climes in a nostalgic way and wanting to quit. Rehabilitation too needs more time, if it is to happen at all. I don't like my environment as yet and really feel lonesome and a terrible need for a woman's love. But she is so far away.

Now that I have written, don't be angry with me any more and keep writing or 'wrighting' – as you would have it spelt – in spite of my occasional silence, which is never devoid of love for you. Thanks for the thought for my birthday and for tobacco. Hope Ravi Shankar brings it.

If you can come, for how long can you come?

I need to do a lot of other work and save money right from now, if I want to see you there next summer. Many many sweet sweet kisses,

Habib

I was still abroad at this point and it made me yet more determined not to stay stuck out on a limb. It was becoming clear to me that it seared my heart to leave Habib in India on his own for a long time – or anywhere else, come to think of it. I decided I should go back to England as soon as I could decently extricate myself, get myself into a bedsitter probably in London, and take up some useful training, which would enable me to earn a living. I knew my parents would support me in a move that appeared so sensible. The one that struck me as most obvious was that of a secretarial course. I had heard you could always get a job if you knew how to type and do shorthand, even if you were pretty bad at spelling, which I was. Moreover, it was what a lot of girls took up and it certainly seemed to stand them in good stead, so why not me? This is exactly what I did, and looking back, it turned out to be one of the most useful decisions I ever made in my life, though it seemed a bit of a random choice at the time. My idea was to take up a job as soon as I was trained, save up money and go to India by road, there being much to see on the way. Luckily for me, computers weren't around and there was nowhere near the present-day range of difficult equipment to master. Manual typewriters were all we had to learn touch-typing on, and we took dictation down in a notebook.

The course itself was very arduous, but focusing on the end result of being employable, I managed to get through it. The very first job I got was fascinating and seemed to be linked to my own interests, if a little remotely. I was taken on by Lady Pamela Hicks as her secretary in her very lavish flat in London, and was required to answer letters of condolence she had received on the death of her mother, Lady Pamela Mountbatten, the wife of the viceroy of India. While doing so, I was inspired to do some research of my own into the way of life of these people to whom I was typing letters, many of them eminent upholders of the British Raj. My readings undoubtedly provided me with a dramatically different picture of life in India from the description that Habib was sending me. Nevertheless, spurred on by all the varying images and so far undaunted, I carried on with my plans for a journey by road, equally enthusiastic about seeing the rest of the world on the way.

There were organizations that took you across the world by bus and truck and it all sounded very exciting, if hazardous. I loved the thought of such an adventurous journey, and went about organizing a loan from Margareta who encouraged me and fully understood my desire to go. I exchanged letters with other members of the road trip being planned, who I began to know a little. They sounded wonderfully friendly and fearless, all of which I wrote about to Habib. I pored over maps, tracing this massive journey with my finger and imagining all the extraordinary countries I would pass through. At the same time, I wondered how many stomach upsets I might have to deal with, as I'd heard this was all part and parcel of life travelling around Asia.

Ages passed before I got a reply to my many lively descriptions – seven months in fact – and by that time I was quite sure he'd either found someone else to fall in love with, or had dwindled into a heap of paralysed misery.

First I received a telegram from him, followed by a letter.

12.5.59
(Naya Theatre address on back of envelope)

Jill darling,
There is no woman. I am a celibate and keep thinking of you. You have a large heart and I expect you would forgive me again – but my silence really meant nothing. It was just one of those things. In fact, many weeks ago, I launched upon writing a very long letter to you, but it was left off in the middle and I had to abandon it eventually because of the cost – but I will complete it and send it some other time. I sent that telegram because I thought the last date of your application for the trip to India was pretty close and there was no time for a letter to get to you. Yes, it was expensive and I had to borrow money. I was horrified to imagine you in India mainly for me, and me in Europe, and both missing one another. Because Germany had asked

me to produce the Indian classic in September, I was to take 3 months for the production and linger on for a month or so here and there. But now they write to me saying that they have ever so many important and unavoidable assignments and festivals, foreign visits and so on this year; so would I be willing to visit in February 1960. That is awful, as far as your plans are concerned. Even for me, it is very unpleasant. Perhaps it is too late for you to try to come to India, though I wish you would still try and that you succeeded. Do, do let me know if it is possible.

I have left my job. Now I am looking for a living and for a house to live in. At the same time I have formed a new theatre group called the New Theatre and got a friend to lend me his garage for rehearsals and started rehearsing three of my own one-act plays.

Meanwhile, my mother is very ill and I must go home leaving this to others for a time, but I have not a penny. You hinted about my pounds some time ago. I think if I had them, I would certainly clear up my debts. But as things stand, your father is right. I don't expect to pay him the fiver in another five years. You see for a long time, the Govt. of India did not transfer my money to my bank in London but insisted they would let me have the amount in rupees here in India.

They began to question whether any money was due to me at all, because they said if you had earned during your stay in Europe, then that amount must be deducted from my scholarship. Anyhow, I do not know how long this correspondence would go on and what the result would be. So you see darling I am not quite as rich, stingy and unscrupulous as I might appear. Conditions in India are terrible and I am forced to selling some of my things.

15.5.59 continued:

My experiment was successful and I think it has shown a definite new way in theatre. But at the moment I have received a personal setback. I have not the same facilities to carry on my experiment still further. The Hindustani Theatre set-up does not have the vision – while here in my own set-up I have all the freedom of artistic expression but no resources or very few. I have to collect donations for my amateur organization. I have collected about £40 so far but we need much more. It is difficult to draw talent for amateur work and much more difficult to get girls to act. It is difficult to do all this without a job and more difficult to find a job that leaves you enough time for theatre. There are many other nasty things but writing about them would be wasting your time and boring you. The artist class of New Delhi is a class of opportunists full of greed, egotism, selfishness, jealousy and destructive revenge-fulness. They are hand-maidens of a few rich women who dominate the cultural field of Delhi – social climbers who use theatre as a stepping stone for personal triumphs. The result is that I am thrown out on the street literally and my creation is virtually thrown to dogs. The irony is that you can't do a damn about it. But you haven't the interest or the energy for revenge. You secretly yearn for peace so as you begin work from scratch but even this peace is denied you. Then you want to retire to the Himalayas. Then is your demoralization complete though it is not certain if the world could really leave you alone even then. Thus more than half your life you are busy trying to defend yourself without cause, or reacting, reacting, reacting to all sorts of stuff and nonsense. You are lucky if in the midst of all this you can take yourself in hand again for a moment to realize that you are losing the purpose of life and that life is losing all its meaning for you. Suddenly then you think of the minimum function of life – the animal function – procreation – and it is hopeless indeed when you feel that you are not fulfilling even the vegetable purpose of life. You think of love and see it is nowhere around. You have neglected it as well and not availed of it. You write a depressing letter to a girl with a stout faith because she has not yet gone through so much. And strangely that girl's faith appears able to nourish you and give you hope and strength again if you are not too far gone already. That girl is you. And I don't think I am too far gone. Love

Habib

As a result of that telegram and the letter, my plans to come to India had to be entirely scrapped, and since they were in such an advanced state it came as a terrific shock. I was extremely deflated by yet another hitch in our arrangements, and I think I had no more ideas as to what I could do to bring comfort to Habib's troubled existence – nor to my own, for that matter. I had wanted to reach him so badly and, yet again, muddles in timing had got in the way. I didn't have the energy nor the means to start making plans again and couldn't think what to write back to improve matters.

Another matter in his letter worried me, Mukti – the monies he refers to. And I feel so ashamed when I read this with you. The fiver my father had lent Habib when he came to stay at the farm is probably worth about ten times as much now, say about £50, so it wasn't that small an amount, but it became a very embarrassing feature in the tangled web of our family relationships. Mainly this was because I knew very well that if Habib didn't pay it back, my father would deem him dishonest, 'typical' of a foreigner in that you couldn't trust them, and question why the hell he had ever thought of lending out that money in the first place. It was likely to remain an 'issue', as my father often made generous gestures, then changed his mood and wanted to retract. Awful really, when you think of how much wealthier we were as a family, compared to Habib's situation. I don't remember if that wretched fiver ever got paid back, or if I handed one to my father saying it was from Habib, when it wasn't. Whatever happened, it did eventually stop being mentioned, so something must have been done.

Apart from some fragile indications that a new theatre might be about to be born, this was a very frustrating spell, one that kept even me quiet.

> NAYA THEATRE
> 135, M-BLOCK, CONNAUGHT CIRCUS, NEW DELHI-1
> TELEPHONE: 45348
> 22-8-59
>
> Jill Love,
> I feel foolish complaining about your silence. Yet I feel it is not mere tit for tat that makes keeps you silent. I hope you are well. But won't you write?

I am going in for some expense in writing on this paper, not because I want to tire you with a lengthy account but merely in order to show off to you the new letter-head of my theatre. Of course you can see it is a poor theatre but I can say now that it is there. (The difference between printed air-letters and an ordinary letter by air is very great in India — and I am earning nothing you see.)

Part of June and July I was away on the hills — middle Himalayas they are called. Took a small play to a hill station — then went on a course — took a week's drama course to earn something. Used the money for hiking. Jolly interesting. We were 3 boys. Walked about 150 miles, climbed about 13000′ — snow, hail storms & all that — just like south of Europe — Pine trees, their smell & all.

On return, I got busy in preparing 3 short plays for a programme shown on 8 & 9 August for Kashmir Flood Sufferers. Worked day & night. We I had to do everything ourselves from ticket-printing, pasting of posters & selling tickets to set-making & arranging the stage. The greatest burden was on me since I have no other job to do. But this is no job — I mean there is no money in it yet. We have not yet finished up with it — we are still busy settling accounts now. But the shows were good, though the plays were terribly under-rehearsed for want of time and proper attention. We made some profit, which is astounding. And now I am busy preparing for the next production — Molière's 'Bourgeois Gentleman' — to be shown on 4th. Nov.

A Story for Mukti 143

I am terribly tired & unhappy. What else. You can't even manage to take a week off from this wretched place because there is a young organisation ~~batch~~ — 3 months old — to be run by just one man — unemployed, half-starved & overworked. If he leaves it even for a while, its death is more or less certain. Besides, where is the money. Hardly time even to earn it. Some journalism ~~things~~ now & then might fetch a meal a day but hardly cigarettes. There is no room; so I sleep on floor in office premises. This is the fourth place we are occupying. From the one the three we have been hunted out. Even here sabotage is being tried. Oh, it is a wretched country. They tried hard to sabotage the show, drove off our actresses. Anyhow, we had the show and even made some money, which is fantastic. There is difficulty of finance for plays always. But why am I writing all this. Yes, I said I was unhappy. But not because of these difficulties. I was a bit hurt because a girl whom I had grown fond of did not come to see my show even after promising — and she is a very good actress. She ended off a good few months' friendship so casually & abruptly. She is a good serious-minded girl — a student — went to Bombay to spend 3 months' vacations — came back & said she does not see any end to this, so has decided to break it off — but she was to come to see the show & didn't. It might sound odd to you — my writing like this to you — but I ~~am~~ am upset & not able to get over it. And I feel I must write this to you. It is silly I know — ~~because~~ it must be some such thing as ~~some~~ pride hurt or something — what I am unable to get over is — the show — of a friend — and she — oh well — to hell with it.

~~23.8.59~~ 27.8.59 — Meanwhile I got your letter. (Note my new address). Oh, I am glad you are still there — & you still think about me. — that's a nice feeling. You

> are so far Jill — you must have grown — & changed — & I still think of you as you were. In a flash, I thought of Devonshire, Bristol & Dartington — and missed England tirelessly. Sometimes I feel so sick of this country & my life of drudgery here that I feel like running away to the mountains — a monk — a monk that I already am — this "more thing, holy" — or go abroad, settle down comfortably & never return. What's the use of complaining Jill darling, about my changing mind when it all depends upon changing circumstances. My god, if you were here with me, what's a would I ever have done to make you a bit happy except give you that intangible, worthless object called love. It would hardly have filled your stomach though. But forgive me all the same. I am looking forward greatly to my coming trip. You have no idea. Wish I could undertake it at once. Really. Well, Jill, I think of you ever so often — & dearly — but nevertheless I hope, love, you are not such a fool as to wait for me, really wait I mean. I am not a man worth waiting for. Sweet Jill. But I send you all my love for what it is worth. Yours, Habib.

Of course, I was still waiting for him, though severely rattled by having to cancel my journey. The time since we had last seen each other had gone very slowly for me – it was full of dreams and plans of somehow getting to India so that we could at last spend some proper time together. It had been a wonderful relief getting into action and planning the journey – that was now not to be. But even as I was very touched by his longing for my company and his missing of England, I did not see his plans for coming to Europe, Germany specifically, as anything to pin my hopes on.

By now, I knew in my heart that Habib had to be in India to develop his ideas and properly use his talents, and I believe that at some level he also knew this was his destiny. Accordingly, his letters start to convey his worries about how to accommodate me and his feelings for me at the same time as being so involved in his work – work that was bound to claim his entire attention. Of course, I didn't know then of the significance of the Naya Theatre letterhead – nobody knew this was to be the beginning of a commitment that would last the rest of his life and would establish authentic Indian folk theatre as a recognized art form. How extraordinary that it should all begin so humbly, rehearsing in a garage!

You asked me, Mukti, how I felt about his being so upset by the girl who had rejected him, and I honestly don't think I was worried other than about the fact that he seemed so unhappy. Feeling jealous or put out would have been out of place, for I was not there to do anything about him. We were friends after all, as well as lovers, and such sadness naturally distressed me and added to my feelings of helplessness. The loneliness he was suffering, I had suffered too – it was all so unbearable and I wouldn't wish it on anyone.

New Delhi - 11.9.59

My dearest Jill,
I got your beautiful gift about a week ago – along with your sweet note (with the intriguing German address on top) dated 8th July 59. Unfortunately I did not meet your nice friend, who brought the charming things. She left a note of apology. I got a wonderful surprise not at all in time; for the man at the Modern Studios to whom it was delivered about a month or so ago, said he clean forgot all about it. In a way though, it was miraculously in time, for it was handed over to me just on the eve of my show of 2 short plays (written and directed by me – I acted in one as well)

suddenly forced upon us on the 5th of Sept. with a very short notice. So after the premiere of what did not turn out to be a terribly exciting performances, though mercifully tolerably (or tolerantly – still better) received, four of us – the most important members of the group – among them a girl, got together and drank whiskey and supped and sipped of that exciting flask you sent me. We loved it and blessed you for turning our evening into a most pleasurable one. I am all the more actively looking out for a room where I can display my cherished possessions now hidden away.

I am sorry for my last letter which was a very stupid one I think. Well, all I can do now is to ask you to forget it – it was written in one of those moods you know.

Well, to be frank, my life even today is not exactly glorious; and how can one help a certain touch of sadness in one's attitude to everything, if one is terribly alone. Then a sudden nostalgia possesses you – nostalgia for distant love – and you begin to live in a mixed atmosphere of Past and Future cut out from the Present – not at all a happy feeling. It would be compensation indeed if work proved rewarding. So far, it seems too early even to say there is a hope. The next 6 months, for which I am here in this awful place, should enable me to decide whether I should not plan to leave this country for good when I do leave it.

In myriad images you come before my mind's eye ever so frequently. Is that a happy thing? No. Can't speak about it all in a letter. But what is it that you want to write to me but did not. And just how do you feel about the whole thing darling. Can you visualize the future? Show me a glimpse of it, won't you. Yours may be a happier vision.

Well, a thousand little kisses everywhere for the flask.

Hab.

13.9.59 I spent the quietest possible birthday. Half of it remains. I expect it to pass just as peacefully. Wonder what exactly you may be doing just at this moment.

14th Suddenly the birthday turned out to be too noisy towards evening. Some friends gave a surprise. But after 36 you do not move towards youth, do you? Ah well, I should like to see you before I am 37 anyway.

The envelope tells me that this letter was forwarded to me at a time when I was staying with my beloved grandmother in London. You never met her, Mukti, for she had already died long before you were born. She took her role as a granny to us all very seriously, and was just the right person to be with – wise and patient, with her feet absolutely on the ground. At one point, when I had earnestly conveyed to her my restlessness and despair over the state of my heart, she looked at me steadily over her specs and said: 'This love affair you are having with the Indian chap will not go away, you know. You will have to sort it out sooner or later.' And of course she was right. Her words echoed perfectly my own feelings in response to Habib's question about how I envisaged our future. Somehow or other, a resolution had to be found.

I want to tell you more about Granny at this point, Mukti, because she was a very central figure to all of us in the family, and has influenced many of us ever since. She often took an unusual moral stand, backed up by great intelligence and warmth of heart. I only have to remember her to sense her natural order and stability, yet she wasn't conventional, not in the least. It was to her that I often turned when in difficulty because you could talk to her about anything, and so long as you didn't set out to shock, she would listen most attentively with a calm, open mind. Her background was most unusual. Born Christabel Harmsworth in 1876, she was the youngest and favourite sister of Alfred Harmsworth, who was later to become Lord Northcliffe, the newspaper baron who established the concept of newspapers as we know them today. She came from a huge Victorian family of thirteen children who lived in London in great poverty, I mean really great. I don't think their father – a brilliant Irish lawyer, but given to much drinking – earned properly at all.

I recently saw a history programme on television about early twentieth-century Britain where Lord Northcliffe was briefly featured. It told of his mother having to wrap him up in newspaper to keep him warm as a baby, when they were living in St John's Wood in a very small flat, penniless. As well as being a great character, Granny could relate some wonderful stories about the family. One I remember particularly was about her two older brothers, Alfred and Harold, who as children shared a winter coat because they couldn't afford one each. The two of them didn't go out together when it was very cold because of that. To help the family finances, one brother would often take 'The Coat', as it was called, off its hook and saunter off to Hampstead Heath to wager wrestling matches with other boys, while encouraging any likely bystander to place bets on the winner. On returning home, usually having gained a few pennies, he would hang up 'The Coat', and the other brother would take his turn to wear it for the next fighting sortie. There was, clearly, an impressive entrepreneurial streak in both brothers even at that young age! Just as well, for their father was to die young of liver failure, leaving a huge brood close to destitution.

There is a touching photo in a book called *The Great Outsiders* by S.J. Taylor where the future Lord Northcliffe is shown as a young man, standing to the side of a motley group of family; twelve-year-old Granny is there too, at their father's funeral in 1888. He looks forlorn, and the caption reads: 'Alfred, wearing the grey travelling suit his brothers and sisters helped him to buy; now everything depended upon him.' For, as the eldest son, the future of the family was his responsibility.

Shortly after this occasion in their early twenties, Alfred and Harold (who later became Lord Rothermere) borrowed a small sum of money and set about revolutionizing the idea and content of the daily newspaper. It made them an absolute fortune, so Granny's life leaped from great poverty to considerable wealth, allowing her to do many things of interest to her, mostly in the region of social reform.

It was she, with her imaginative and uncluttered approach to life, who eventually made it possible for me to set off for India, offering me the fare to go on a P&O liner, on a route that is blocked today – through the Suez Canal and across the Red Sea. And there were no strings attached; it was a wonderful gesture that I was only too glad to accept. Granny's money mostly came from Lord Northcliffe, so in a way, he is also to be thanked.

New Delhi 2.12.59

Jill love,
I feel guilty again for silence. And you wrote such flattering nice letters. I was immersed in Moliere, finished 3 days ago. I write this during the short spell I got before plunging into the same play again to be prepared again with a new cast. The last performance was prepared for a college with college boys and teachers. It was important for me in many ways and proved very popular.

My silence is also due to the fact that I am tending to be a bore. My problems haven't changed a bit – have only worsened. Having hardly anything else on mind, what is one to write about?

I want to show Moliere's 'Bourgeois Gentleman', a musical comedy – again with a new cast by February and leave India by April. I think I would go straight to German (Rostock) for 3 months before I start moving around. I haven't heard from Rostock for a long time. So I am writing to them for my ticket today. I hope nothing has gone wrong. But if something has, I am in a mood to reconcile to any darned fate. I have an offer of a good role in a film but I am considering whether or not to accept it.

Momentarily I am well off for some time now. Because I got my scholarship money from the Govt. of India. But you see they did not give me any part of it in pounds, for which I was fighting for so long. And the exchange problems in India being as difficult as they have become of late, I do not know what I shall do when I visit London during my trip. Worst fate of all, it also means your five pounds are doomed after all unless I have bright prospects of a living in London when I come. Even the Indian money would hardly last me up to March if I remain unemployed still.

What the hell have you gone and done Jill. Whatever it is, for God's sake do not remain divided about the wretched thing inside you. It is so painful. I know it is easier said. I have been through it many times myself. And what gave you the idea I am clear-headed in such matters. I think quite frankly I am quite stupid about them. Yet thank you for the lovely thought. It was so pleasing for its sincerity. But to come back to it again, how is it with you now? Do write.

I have been a monk for a long time and don't even feel the need for love. Creative work is wonderful. It only costs you your weight.

We have long been out in the street again – our theatre I mean. We were asked to leave our last place too. I put up with a friend 7 miles off from town. As long as I don't have a proper address, you may use the same old one.

I met Balwant twice very briefly since he returned a few days ago. He came to see my play and then I ran into him today. I am lunching with him tomorrow. I expect he would talk a lot about you. He was talking about you a little today.

Heaps of love and all my best wishes for a merry Xmas, Jill darling – and a very Happy New Year. A kiss. HT

I have been thinking hard about what I might have done that Habib asks about. It is annoying that I tended to make oblique references to important matters which he wasn't able to grasp completely, and today, nor am I. But carefully digging into my memories and looking at the date of his letter, I am reminded that it was three months before my twenty-first birthday in March 1960. A few months before, I had met John, a friend of my cousin, and had found him interesting. He was a tall and willowy young man who had visited Granny's house when I was staying there, and I had been asked to join them for tea. His background was unusual – he was the son of a famous English film actor – and he was very pleasant to meet and rather glamorous.

We went out for a few months, tentatively and rather shyly, but I think neither of us had much idea of what we were doing or why we were doing it. I guess we were just lonely and looking for love. The whole thing worried me, for at that time, John was going through a religious phase. Many young people went in for spells of religious passion in the 1950s and '60s – it was quite fashionable to do so. The religion he was involved in was, at least to me, very obscure. It was called Subud, and I've got to say I didn't understand a word of what he believed in, or where it was supposed to lead. I just knew it made him look very solemn and distant. I was also very torn because I missed Habib greatly. Yet so many difficulties seemed to race into view whenever I contemplated our relationship that I was beginning to wonder if anything could ever work out between us. I must have written to Habib in my annoyingly oblique way to try to unburden myself of these conflicts.

As it happened, the outcome of this small flurry was that John eventually went off with my best friend, Annabel, who I had met during my secretarial course and who was very beautiful. He did this right in the middle of my twenty-first birthday party, which was held at her mother's house. So there was humiliation indeed – to be left so visibly alone on such an important date, crying in the bathroom!

It has occurred to me since that it is often the rather tenuous romances that hurt most when they end, not the really good ones which have offered much in terms of affection and happiness. This is odd. You would think it would be the other way around. What also interests me at this point is how Habib and I confided in each other concerning the ups and downs of other relationships. No, not the ups, but the downs at least. Had we written of the joys we were experiencing in the contexts of other involvements, I think we would have both been very much dismayed. The bad bits we passed on, I guess, because they indicated we were still available for each other and still friends, while the good bits were tactfully not alluded to.

The Balwant that Habib refers to in his letter is someone without whom this story might never have unfolded as it did. It was about two months earlier that a remarkable chance meeting took place in London – one that was to make a big difference to my thinking and my future. I had a cousin, Josephine, who had lived and worked in Kenya. All of a sudden and with very short notice, she asked me to a party that she was giving for a group of Kenyans who were attending what was grandly called 'The Lancaster House Conference', where they were hoping to finalize arrangements for Kenya's coming of independence. It was not a smart party, I was surprised to find; it was held in her hot little sitting room, somewhere in the region of Tuffnel Park. When I first entered I couldn't see a thing as the room was so dark, but the music was loud and lively, shapes were dancing cheek to cheek and other shapes were sitting on chairs placed around the walls. I sat on one of these chairs and thought I'd talk to whoever was sitting next to me. The conversation, which was more or less shouted, went like this:

'Hello. I don't know anyone here. Do you?'

'No. I have just come from India. I know no one at all.'

'Which part of India are you from?'

'I come from Delhi.'

'Really! I know someone in Delhi who's a writer – he works in a theatre there.'

'Is it Habib Tanvir that you know?'

'Yes. Why? Do you know him?'

'Yes, indeed. He saw me off at the airport a fortnight ago. You must be Jill. He has told me about you. Your voice is just as he described it.'

I laughed and he added, 'And your laughter too.'

And that was all it took.

After such a revelation I saw nothing more of the Lancaster House gathering, for we simply talked and talked, moving into a quieter corner to do so. The person I bumped into so fortuitously was Balwant Gargi, a writer and friend with whom Habib had both lived and worked. He had come to the party by chance: he'd heard about it from a guest at the same hotel where he was staying, and decided to tag along because he didn't know how to occupy himself that evening. I asked him if he thought Habib really was anxious for me to come to India. His reply was unequivocal: Habib was very keen to see me in India and had told his mother about me. This meant he was serious and I should plan an India trip.

While this made me very happy, I had to know how I would survive financially as I could not depend on Habib to keep me going. How difficult was it to get a job? Balwant was reassuring. If I could type I could come and work as a secretary for him – of course I could type by now – and there was a spare room where I could stay in his house, recently vacated by Habib. This was all unbelievably positive. And since the precarious nature of Habib's arrangements made me doubt he would soon get back to Europe, I knew it was up to me to make the effort. Over the next few days I thought of little else but how to organize a journey – by ship this time – from Southampton to Bombay.

132, M. Block Connaught Circus, New Delhi
23.3.60

Jill love,
I shan't be there this summer. Rostock theatre writes to me their Ministry had not yet finalised negotiations. So there. I don't know whether this means postponement merely or cancellation altogether. I should hope the former. I have written to them to clarify. At the same time, I am heart broken. At no time of my life – to write about the negative aspect of it – had I wanted so much to escape from my country and its problems as just at this time. For the same reason perhaps it is not so bad after all. At least, so I console myself.

Innumerable little conflicts were raging in my mind for some time past causing a complete deadlock in activity, a state of irksome indecision in general resulting in escape (I am not explaining my unforgivable silence Jill darling, please; about this I only want you to be generous again and forgive me) I can't begin to write about these conflicts. They cover such a long range, including you – my life past and future, my work, hopes, plans.

hundreds of thoughts covering success, failure, values, way of life etc. This society is still terribly backward. For the great majority of individuals, it has failed to provide the bare necessities of life. There is a terrible lack of spiritual content in the human life of today. Society needs to be turned upside down, inside out, and to be completely renovated after a good spanking on the bottom. We are all lazy and indifferent not to bend every effort in that direction. Whereas I consider my generalisation is justified and not merely subjectively inspired, I am at the same time avoiding the still more tiresome comment on my personal experiences. If you remember what I wrote a year ago, you don't need to know anything further.

I escaped into rummaging through all my old papers, MS, letters, books. It took weeks cataloging about 600 books and dumped them in a library in order to ensure them against worms. Have planned out work for summer: revision and publication of old plays for adults, children, selection of poems for a book, writing of a new play which I have outlined. At present I am revising an old play of mine in order to produce it again and show it by the first week of May. In April, I organise an exhibition of theatre brochures and photos of Europe – about 300. I did a small play for TV recently; am now preparing to do another; and planning to write articles. March 28th is 'Id' – a kind of Muslim Christmas – for which I wanted to go home. But home being 800 miles, I have postponed the trip to May.

It is funny neither to be able to leave this country nor to be able to live here properly, with economic, spiritual and emotional stability. It is a delightful chaos. One need not moan about it. But one feels terribly self-conscious and guilty if one did not write about it – did not write about the most important personal feelings. On the other hand, one feels guilty writing. You deserve a more cheerful letter – one may be aware of it and yet not be able to help it. You have a genius for writing with such brevity and full of joy – giving strength.

Friends bring joy on all levels. This however, does not bring stability, the source of happiness. Half of my heart is in this country. Half outside it. It is terrible. I don't know when this gets resolved and integrated. I give it 3 or 4 to 6 months. There.

Balwant has gone to Bombay for some weeks. I may act in a play of his, which he is getting translated from Punjabi into Hindi.

Part of the summer I spend at Norah Richard's hermitage in a valley of the lower Himalayas. There – a woman of 85 – she lives the life of a recluse. I was with her last year, you remember? (An Englishwoman, who rendered great service to the cause of Indian drama.) She resembles you in a remarkable way – physically as well as in disposition and a simple, clear approach to life. Her picture of youth reminds me of you so often. It is at her place at Kangra, where I intend to write my play. I spent Christmas too with her and it was at this time and in this place I got the idea for this play. The place and Norah inspired it. It has much to do with Norah herself and her 'retreat'. It is a satire – in a light vein – about theatre conditions in this country.

What are your plans for the summer, Jill? I hope you make some wonderful plans and enjoy yourself in a wonderful way. Can you send me a small photo of yours so I know how much more mature you look now.

Don't curse me for not coming. This might be very upsetting but they informed me so darned late. This when I inquired – after a long and strange state of suspense. They were surprised. They referred to an older letter they said they wrote to me, which I never got. I am hoping they call me next autumn.

I wonder if you would like to meet Begun Zaidi's daughter, Shama Zaidi. She paints. She is in some school in London. If you would care to meet her, I could obtain her address and write to her to contact you perhaps. She is a very nice girl, victimised by an awful mother.

Sometimes I get an irresistible desire to start on a long journey to look at my country, to find out why it is so bad. That would be the nicest escape from realities of life. But this strange country makes even that an almost impossible task to undertake unless you have heaps of gold.

With heaps and heaps of love in which I am never poor, Jill dearest

Yours, Habib

Norah Richards has always fascinated me ever since Habib described her as a kindred spirit, as it were, even though I was still young and she very old. I have since read quite a lot about her and am proud of the fact that Habib thought I resembled her in spirit – a generous comparison to say the least. She was unique and dedicated, completely avant-garde in her attitude towards British India and duly revered for the huge amount of encouragement she gave Indian artists, writers and dramatists who stayed in her mountain retreat. She was practical as well as visionary, providing a venue in which they could live and work, rather like the Elmhursts of Dartington who I've described earlier.

The rest of the letter, I must say, is full of disturbing ripples, but nothing compared to the veritable tsunami that blew in with the next.

Raipur 28.5.60

My sweetest Jill
Thanks for that lovely picture and the great news that you are visiting India. Apologies for the belated thanks. Once more that is.

This is terrible. Terrible that even though one is constantly and acutely thinking of writing nearly every day from the moment one received the lovely news, still it should actually be ages before one got down to it; I might merely mention that I am aware that no one's patience is inexhaustible and that one day my negligence might just amount to too much. Not yet I pray you though Jill. No love, it was just carelessness – carelessness of the worst order. I am writing this with a shocked feeling that soon summer would be over – time for you to be here – when do you plan to be here; for how long; are you not leaving it open; what programme, I mean itinerary or is there one at all yet. I am able to write now because I am home for one thing. I have come home for Id – a festival – for 2 weeks – and shall be back in Delhi on the 9th. But it is a pity that I am not able to enjoy the peace that is here – as much as I would like to. This, because I have brought so much Delhi work with me.

This is a new work. A new professional theatre. Mark my address. This is employment after one full year's complete unemployment. I am to produce four plays per year for them. It is a year's contract to start with and that is as much as I am interested in at the moment. So I am now looking for my new team of actors. This involves correspondence and interviews with scores of people.

At first when I heard you are coming, I vaguely thought it really was possible perhaps to see India with your eyes – i.e., to be with you in your travels a bit. But this new assignment might just keep me glued to Delhi for one whole year at least. This thought is disturbing.

There are other disturbing thoughts. My life is quite disturbed nowadays – specially the last couple of months or so. It is a strange conflict. I am living with a girl whom I like but not quite love. The fondness just lacks that one little spark – passion. So I call it an involvement. I call it this because this feeling is not mutual. So I feel weak and angry with myself.

Sometimes I resign and lull my thoughts; at others I am just horribly disturbed for not knowing how to end it. But I shall not pour out all my worries at one go. One of the principal ones of them is over – that of a job, though that deprives me of my freedom a bit. That's why I have cancelled the Kangra trip. I got the job about 5 weeks ago – on the same day on which I lost my job last year.

> *I am busy with my paper work and actually quite thrilled about my new assignment. Begum Zaidi's viciousness however against me is still the same. That reminds me. Here is her daughter's address:*
> *Miss Shama Zaidi,*
> *109, Constantine Road, Hampstead, NW3*
> *You are looking just the same in that snap Jill – a bit sobered perhaps, more mature, but still quite as innocent, and charming as ever. I like your new hair. I owe you one of mine now. But by then you might snap me yourself.*
>
> *That would be unfair though. If I can get one from Balwant, I would send you. He has a good one but he has become so elusive. He is alright though actually.*
>
> *I am all eyes for you. Write to me at once when you are due. I would suggest you came here in October if you want to avoid the terrible heat, though of course October for me is the worst month for the amount of work that is bound to keep me bogged down to it. But soon you should be able to see 2 plays by me and then I would have more time too.*
>
> *Love and kisses.*
> *Habib*

Even the handwriting was wild, not clear and controlled as it was in the others. It was difficult to know what to make of Habib's situation, but without a doubt, it filled me with dread. To have little love affairs in one's life en route, as it were, is one thing, but to actually set up house with someone, to live with them where you are based, is quite another. And simultaneously to plan a reunion with someone else dear to your heart, who you have yearned to meet for a long time – how could this possibly work out? In addition, to be in a state of paralysis when it comes to making decisions and taking action – that is surely confirmation of confusion to come. Looking back, I can see that Habib was a lot more able to live with emotional stress than I could bear. I have wondered about this: how could he possibly put up with the amount of tensions that often gathered around him, without bursting forth into decisive action or having a breakdown? For myself, such turmoil right on one's doorstep would be too much to bear. But not so him; when he saw no way of gaining control over his complicated personal life, he escaped into his creative work, and it was a marvellous escape, taking him out of himself and away into a different mental landscape as nothing else could. Mention of plays and productions always increased at such times, as they did now.

But for myself, what was I to do, with plans for travel well advanced and my whole heart, yet again, set on this journey? Having dreamt of being in India with Habib for so long, I think I just blundered on, hoping for the best, relying more and more on Balwant to make proper arrangements for my visit, waiting to see what was to happen.

The Delhi Playhouse,
869 East Park Road,
New Delhi – 5
26.8.60

My dearest Jill,
I hope I am writing to you just in time to get you just before you leave UK.

I feel awful for the delay again. Of course I was busy but I curse myself for not having will and energy enough to sit down and put pen and paper together earlier – though I thought of you continually.

I got Balwant to take a snap of mine. After great persuasion I succeeded. But he took his own time again in developing it. At last, he told me it was ruined. So here is another taken last year in winter. It is different. I look a bit thinner still, for I think I have lost weight, though perhaps gained wisdom!!!

I believe you touch Bombay in the first week of September. Well that is not far off now. How long do you intend to stay in Bombay? I don't want you to plan too tightly when you don't wish it. But Bombay deserves not less than a week. What I do want to tell you however is this; I am playing 'Aurangzeb' (The last great Moghul emperor of India) in Dryden's 'Aurangzeb' to be performed on an improvised open-air stage in a Delhi garden from the 13th October upto the 20th. It is being produced by Michael Stephens, a BBC representative here. It would have Indian music and dances as well. I should be very glad if you could be here in time to see this. In case you want to read the play in advance, you can obtain the Penguin book called John Dryden – a Penguin Poets' Series – in London.

My own 2 plays, my productions I mean, are coming off by the middle of November. They of course would be in Urdu. Of these you would see rehearsals as well as shows.

I am afraid by the time you get here I shall have lost much more weight at this rate. I only hope you would be able to recognise me.

I am terribly excited about your coming and I wait breathlessly. There is such a lot to say but I shall withhold it. Its proper time is now when you are here. So till we meet – my best love and many kisses.

Yours Habib

My anxieties were not eased by this letter. I hardly knew what to expect and had even got to the point of wondering if I should cancel the whole trip, but by this time it had been with me for so long that I couldn't bring myself to give up the idea. Tickets had been bought to go on a small P&O liner with money offered by my Gran and I looked forward enormously to the experience of sailing. However, when it came to it, I barely took in the extraordinary sights and the changing world through which I was passing for three weeks, for I didn't know what to expect at the other end.

I do remember that my cabin contained three nuns who were going to be missionaries in the subcontinent. It was a crowd in that small cabin, and every time I opened the door to take a rest on my bunk they were praying. The door bumped their heels regularly and they would very nearly be catapulted headlong into their beds by my intrusion. This provided some light relief during an otherwise rather strange spell of suspended living, for they were a very good-tempered bunch. One nun, in fact, became my friend. I was interested in knowing why she wanted to be a missionary in India. I particularly noticed that all three of them had cut their hair brutally short and one day I was bold enough to ask her why. She answered that it was because as nuns they didn't want to be too attractive to any prospective converts, which surprised me. I couldn't help feeling this was an awful shame and that they would make more converts if they presented themselves as young and beautiful! By such small, unusual encounters one's mind is diverted.

I also remember the extraordinary experience of going down the Suez Canal which seemed hardly wider than a fairly narrow road, seeing Egyptian families living on either side, fishing and farming and tending their children and animals as we passed by. After this, the climate changed to become extremely hot and humid as we sailed across the Red Sea. On board ship, we were given several extra meals a day and so a lot of time was spent eating, and in the evening, after a huge dinner, we would read on our bunks or dance to live music. Much of this was fun but my heart was not light enough to give myself over to it. One of the sailors on the boat – a handsome Scots engineer – took a great liking to me and tried to persuade me not to join Habib in Delhi, saying it sounded like a plan that would end in tears. He meant well, wishing only to warn me, but I could not bear to listen.

When I arrived in Bombay, I was met by Balwant's friends who were kind and welcoming, and they took me to their flat through streets of chaos and noise, the like of which I had never experienced before. I had my first truly Indian meal which I found delicious, especially as it had taken a very long time to arrive! In the middle of the night, I woke up and turned on my lamp, to find myself surrounded by hundreds of cockroaches that were just sitting on the floor, quite still. I decided not to get out of bed, even though I badly needed to go to the bathroom. Eventually, I had to, and miraculously they all scuttled away. The next day they did not reappear, and anyway I was about to take a train for Delhi.

Looking out of the train window, I felt a comfortable sense of familiarity and began to relax, thinking this was just the place I wanted to be, whatever the future held. I warmed to the sight of villagers in brilliantly coloured clothes crouching in the fields or gracefully walking along tracks with bundles on their heads; of little groups of huts with cows hanging around. Even the smells seemed very familiar, as did the cries of the chai-wallahs bringing kettles and little clay teacups through the train corridors. I was very much at home. Despite any problems that might await me, I was beginning to feel very cheerful and buoyed up that I had finally reached India, Habib's country, and already loved it.

Balwant met me at the Delhi railway station and took me in a rickety old Ambassador taxi to his house near Connaught Circus. This was a brilliantly situated small building shaped like a wedge – it was tucked away out of the traffic but right in the centre of town. The best description I have of it is in a letter I wrote to my granny shortly after I arrived, which was passed back to me after her death.

Dearest Granny,

Got your very welcome letter just now, and as you are at Sanduck, I can send you and the others all the latest news together with these few photographs which are hot from being developed, or cold I should think would be more correct. I had gone to see this old potter only three days ago (Minni Singh of Delhi Blue Pottery). He was absolutely sweet – has given me the name of a book all about Hindu philosophy in a nutshell which he says I must read so that we can then discuss our ideas about things. I was also given some clay to play with and you can see that I have made something in one of the pictures. If you like any of the photos I can get bigger copies.

I have just been to buy a bed from the market, also a mattress. This is because guests have come and my old bed has gone quite rightly to them. Had the most terrific drive back with both bed and mattress stuffed onto a cart (tonga) through the lovely warm evening, the lights sparkling from inside each stall and masses of people moving slowly about. You know, Granny, I am still quite overwhelmed by this country. There is such a lot to see – I simply look and look and look, without ever seeming to get enough. By the way, the bed cost 10/- shillings, a new string one with proper wooden legs, and the mattress 15/-. I went to buy them with the cook who is a miserably built little bloke with tiny sad eyes. He thinks I am just about the biggest joke that ever happened, however, and seems to enjoy these outings where I can't speak a word of Hindi hardly and he certainly doesn't understand English.

I know exactly what you mean when you say for me not to let my instincts, maternal ones that is, run away with me. All the same it is a fact that all my instincts including ones I didn't even know I had, are by this time thoroughly involved. Don't worry though. I am actually very happy, and though you will be surprised to hear it and probably won't believe it, I also feel extremely clear-headed and wise even.

For the last two days I have been away to Agra where the Taj Mahal stands, so I am again continuing this letter to you. It was a lovely trip. I went with an Australian I met in Delhi, and we really did a proper tourist act with cameras and jeans and all the rest of tourist paraphernalia. The Taj was so beautiful. It really has a touch of magic about it. One's breath really is taken momentarily away on seeing it. We stayed in a missionary hostel which was very comfortable. Missionaries are very strange as a breed. The women especially. They all seem to be almost frighteningly jolly, very toughly built with enormous hairy legs and hangy clothes. Anyway, they are doing far the most work here as far as education is concerned, so I suppose one should not mind too much the other things.

I seem to have taken weeks to write this letter to you. This house where I am staying has been such chaos as you would not imagine possible. First some ordinary painters and carpenters came in to do it up for the year, now they have all been fired in the middle of the work for some special fellow to cast a more artistic eye on the set-up, and make it into a sort of 'ideal home'. The court-yard is full of manuscripts, suitcases, and tables and you can hardly get to your own room through it all. I was going to send you photos but they have got lost in all the mess. I shall find them soon and let you have them though.

I think better get this off right away or you will never get it. With much love from Jill

And what of Habib? He appeared the evening following the day of my arrival in Delhi, and hardly looked like the grinning Cheshire Cat person I had so joyfully encountered in England two years before. He didn't seem to be himself, not surprisingly, though friendly and loving. But by the end of the evening he had relaxed enough for us to feel easy together, though much was left unsaid.

It is difficult to write about what happened next, during that first stay in India. There was much happiness at odd moments, for the pleasure we felt in each other's company, and the harmony of our relationship that had kept it alive for so long, were hard to kill. But the context of his situation, where he was actually living with another woman who seriously wanted him, and who was prepared to end her life if she lost him, made it impossible for us to be 'normal'. There were many difficult scenes, and a lot of distress for all of us. The displays of dramatically raw emotion shook my typically English temperament deeply and I found myself wanting to run away. I'm sure you must be thinking how naive I was for not expecting such turmoil, given the circumstances. As it happened I had expected it, but how could I have fully prepared myself for what was to come? As it was, I was shocked to have arrived right in the middle of such strife, and after some weeks, quite exhausted.

I did my work for Balwant – who was much burdened and upset by the drama being acted out around him – and continued to see Habib from time to time, often under chaotic circumstances. Eventually I got ill – and that was enough for me! I could see no resolution coming about in these circumstances and, in addition, I could not see my accommodation remaining stable, with Balwant having to put up with so much. After five very disturbing months I simply booked myself on a flight and took off. I think I'd never felt so sad in all my life, either before or after, as on that flight going back to England. Pure desolation. Habib, worn down by guilt, silent and helpless when I told him I was leaving, looked even more miserable when he came to say goodbye. The last sight of him standing at the airport bus station slowly raising his hand in a half-hearted wave is still painful. I had also made the decision that I didn't want to hear from him again and had told him so, adding that I would not be in touch myself.

6

> The Green Snake — 25 May '63 New York.
>
> Had slept but then again suddenly awakes the brain
> I see again that neither you nor any other by my side
> But the pillow of sorrow wet with the tears of a lonely night
> A rock of pain on heart not to be lifted
> the One blackness astonishingly buried every movement of the eyes
> Every cry of the lone heart, every crease of the lonely bed
> And somewhere in the night's blackness blazing
> The green eyes of a pretty snake made of cloth
> Brought me casually from a shop.
>
>   N.Y. 26 May '63
> Jill darling,
>   Here is the 'Green Snake', which started uncoiling itself in my brain as I returned from the Terminal & walked home. Before 6 P.M. i.e. before your plane had taken off, the poem was complete. So I thought I might send it to you at once.
>   Since composing this I have felt a lot better. And thank heavens for that. For I was miserable as I left you. Unbearably so.
>   I have arranged the green snake on top of the lamp that stands behind the green sofa chair on

Back in England, there followed two years without any further correspondence. I returned to my flat in London – which I shared with three warm-hearted Jewish girls –and took up some temporary secretarial work at the same time as trying to continue with my singing lessons, not that I felt like singing. But my flatmates were wonderful, just what anyone needed after such a fundamental upset. They hugged me when I cried (which was quite often), reassured me that I'd be alright after a bit, and constantly got into troublesome romances themselves upon which subject, with my new-found experience I could offer heartfelt commiserations and advice. We cooked together, endlessly talked, ran out of money but luckily not all at the same time, lent each other pounds to be able to carry on, and generally gave each other much comfort on all levels.

I did not contact Habib. I tried not to think about him. Meanwhile, Balwant wrote to me to say that Habib had married. I was not surprised; in fact, quite relieved that at last he was settled. Then one day, walking back to my flat feeling unusually cheerful, I opened the front door to see, lying on the doormat, a blue airmail letter. With an Indian stamp on the front and the all-too-familiar handwriting. I remember dropping it and how it fluttered to the ground as I tried to open it, for I was trembling and my hands had become suddenly clumsy.

While I had kept Habib's earlier letters in my red writing box, for some reason, Mukti, I seem not to have kept this one. Perhaps it gave me such a shock I didn't know what to do with it and just put it down haphazardly. Anyway, the gist of it was that he was very excited to tell me that he was coming to England soon and then going on to America on another scholarship. Would I come to the airport at such-and-such a time to meet him and please would I keep lots of time free for when we could be together? I was amazed. It had been two and a half years since I had seen or heard from him. Suddenly, it was as if nothing had happened, at least not to him.

What was going on? Was he still so desperate to get out of India? How long was this trip to be? Had his marriage ended so soon?

I consulted my flatmates, of course, who kindly put their heads together to sort out some advice. It ranged from 'Tell him to go to hell' to 'If you don't meet him you'll never know what his situation is or if you've got over him', with several other considerations in between. I can pretty well guess what your advice would have been, Mukti, but you know, had I taken that advice and stuck to it, you simply wouldn't exist! Nor would your mum or your brothers Kim and Willoughby – four people who are so obviously meant to be. Think of that! It's an odd thought – simply not tenable. So you must know that I did go to the airport, I did take up with Habib again and, despite the traumas of the past it was a wonderful reunion, like coming home; quite inexplicably happy and calm. And those feelings lasted throughout our stay in America together (I ended up accompanying him there for six weeks) and persisted in London, where we remained together for many months afterwards.

How could this have been, you may well ask, when I had been so badly let down? It's a very reasonable question, and has given me much thought. I can only say that essentially, deep down, I didn't feel I had been jilted and was no longer loved, even though Habib had married someone else. I had been through so much anguish, but felt that the current that existed so strongly between us had not been switched off. Outwardly, there had been so much change but, inwardly, surprisingly little.

I didn't gather either that Habib felt any differently than he had before, though he had evidently gone through a marriage ceremony. He must have become 'married' eventually, growing into it as a cooperative venture – I'm sure he did – but even then he really didn't seem to change, not cutting himself off in the way that people usually do. He just went on being himself, open to all eventualities. Thinking of some of the insights he gave me about himself, I believe he simply didn't understand what it meant to play a role in real life – husband, father, son – despite his skill in acting them out on stage. He confessed to me that such labels eluded him; they were bewildering and he felt he had little clue as to how to fit himself into them.

I do understand that feeling – that there are expectations and images upheld by society (and not necessarily bad ones either) which you cannot always agree with but are required to conform to. And you aren't able to do that without sensing some falseness in yourself. Then you are called a 'loose cannon' or some such thing for not being able to fit comfortably into normal convention, and not only are you bewildered, so is everyone else. You can gauge whether you are this kind of person if you automatically question what you are told, and also what you are directed to do – especially if it comes via what are called 'the authorities', whoever they may be. There is a pressing need to find out the truth for yourself: you *must* – which means you are an awkward individual who can't fit into a mould. I think there are a few like this in our family and, interestingly enough, they seem to have been born awkward, rather than grown into it.

My nature too contains an element of this and, I would tentatively say, perhaps that's why it was possible to pick up our relationship from where it had left off. It was no good telling myself I should be furious with Habib for the muddles he made and the pain he had caused, for whatever 'should' be, I wasn't. I had been certainly, but that was in the past. In the new 'now',

I couldn't muster up the same feelings of outrage and didn't actually want to. Once I got used to the idea that he was back again, I was delighted that at last we had time to spend together, like an unexpected treat, and wanted to make the best of it.

With his way of letting people be themselves, which is a rare attribute in my experience, Habib was a delight to live with. His main concerns were in his own thoughts and, because he was so absorbed in them, I felt free to get on with mine. This way of going along suited me well enough and made for ease and space between us. As a result, even if we were in the same small flat all day, where he would be writing away and I would be cooking and going in and out to work, we didn't fall over each other or feel claustrophobic in our relationship. So there was a short spell of domesticity, of being relatively settled, Mukti, just a few weeks after he landed in England, which was so unexpected and so harmonious. After that, Habib went off on his lecture tour of America, and according to our arrangement, I followed shortly afterwards.

The first place I had fixed up for myself to stay in America was with a teacher-friend of mine who had a small flat in Harlem. Habib was then busy touring around by plane, giving lectures on theatre, which was part of his scholarship requirements. I stayed for a week with Diane, completely unaware that a young white girl on her own on the streets of Harlem, sometimes at night, was not quite the usual thing – although I did get an inkling of this when I asked a policeman, as you do in England, where a certain street was. He looked amazed and responded rather aggressively, telling me I shouldn't be walking around by myself anyway. He was heavily armed, with pistols bulging, and I came to the conclusion that police in America were very different from those in Britain.

At this point I had one of the most inspiring experiences of my life, which I truly wish Habib could have witnessed. I was asked to sing a couple of solos in the church where my friend, who was a music teacher, played the organ. I didn't realize until I got there that the church was only for black people, and so I found myself the only white person amongst several hundred. I was placed in a gallery above the organ and I had decided to sing a couple of Spirituals which suited my voice very well. Standing so high and filling the whole great edifice with my songs, looking down at this passionately religious crowd below with their wonderful multicoloured hats and uninhibited way of expressing their joy, is something I will never forget. Several hugged me when I appeared amongst the congregation afterwards and asked me to please join their choir. Their warmth was very touching and I wished I could have stayed longer.

Joining Habib turned out to be a complicated business because he had flights booked for him in advance all around the country while I was restricted to buses. There was a strange atmosphere in every bus you got on, as a result of strict segregation – meaning the black people sat in the back, the whites in front. And when we stopped for a break, the queues for drinks and lavatories were also strictly segregated. I got in a muddle in the middle of the night and stood in the 'wrong' queue and was hurried back to the 'right' queue by anxious attendants. My granny had warned me about this as she had been to America some years before, and noted what a bore it all was and how much friendlier the blacks were compared to the whites. I had to agree.

Since Habib was travelling so much faster than myself, I would catch up with him at a lecture venue only now and again in my Greyhound bus while he would have flown in and out of several by that time, giving his talks. I do remember South Carolina, as everywhere I looked the trees were all hung with what looked like dusty cobwebs in the drooping trees, a surprising sight that I had never seen before. We were invited to stay in separate rooms in a homestead where there really was a white wooden balcony supplied with rocking chairs, bourbons that clinked cheerfully with fresh ice, and friendly people (no blacks though, as segregation was still much in evidence in the South) waiting in the warm darkness for Habib's discourse.

This was a meandering affair delivered with enormous style and elegance, its structure no doubt diluted by the generous supplies of whisky and therefore difficult to follow. 'You see,' he explained later. 'I wanted to talk to them clearly of my confusion. Life is confusing – it has so many elements. I think I got through to them.' This was surely true – so concentrated was the atmosphere by the end of the talk – but true in an unusual way. It was as if a spell had been cast on the audience out of which they dragged themselves with difficulty, and it was Habib's charisma that held them enthralled. I doubt if anyone would have remembered much of the talk but the magic of the moment would have stayed with them for a very long time.

After six weeks I had to go back to England, for I had a singing commitment that was important and couldn't be missed. Just before leaving I had passed a shop in New York selling all sorts of strange, exotic artefacts and, coiled up in the window as a decorative element, was a bright green snake made of woven cotton with blazing eyes. It wasn't that heavy or long, so I instantly thought I'd buy it as a memento of this visit – something that Habib could pack in his luggage. What

Jill MacDonald

an odd present! I gave it to him rather hesitantly just before taking a taxi to the airport and he looked at it for a long time, turning it this way and that in his hands. He seemed genuinely fascinated by it.

Shortly after I got back to my flat in London – which felt horribly empty for two of the girls had moved out while I'd been away – this poem came from America.

25th May 1963 New York

> *The Green Snake*
> *Had slept but then again suddenly awakes the brain*
> *   I see again neither you nor any other by my side*
> *   But the pillow of sorrow wet with the tears of a lonely night*
> *   A rock of pain on heart not to be lifted*
> *   One blackness entombing every movement of the eyes*
> *   Every cry of the lone heart, every crease of the lonely bed*
> *   And somewhere in the night's blackness blazing*
> *   The green eyes of a pretty snake made of cloth*
> *   Brought me casually from a shop.*

Jill darling,

Here is the 'Green Snake', which started uncoiling in my brain as I returned from the Terminal and walked home. Before 6 PM i.e., before your plane had taken off, the poem was complete. So I thought I might send it to you at once.

Since composing this I have felt a lot better. And thank heavens for that. For I was miserable as I left you. Unbearably so.

I have arranged the green snake on top of the lamp that stands behind the green sofa chair on a green stand. It is all coiled round the green stand, the gold top bar, and reclining finally on the gold lamp shade; and changes colours as you put on or off the light there. Lighted up, its mouth and eyes on the shade, glare and look ferociously beautiful. I watched it thus from my bed for long – fascinated. Now this snake must remain with me for ever till it gets passed on to posterity, so they can interpret the poem in its light.

Well, and how was the journey? And did you get your baggage easily and get home soon enough without difficulty? Could you sleep in the train? Probably you are already busy writing all this to me.

On return home yesterday I was a bit shocked to learn from Mrs. Kinley's letter that her husband, my host in Pittsburgh, was down with a severe heart attack and has been unconscious for 2 weeks in a hospital. This is my late friend's old father. It is so sad and such a pity. I wondered a bit whether now I should go to Pittsburgh at all; but eventually decided I should. So I go tomorrow. I do hope I get a talk and get paid for it well enough to cover my hotel expenses there. I also hope Jacksonville has a talk too for me.

> *Oh what a lovely time we spent together here. I am really glad I am going away for a while now. I need to. I expect to get your letter either in Jacksonville (forwarded to me) or on my return here,*
>
> *Lots of love,*
> *Habib*

I loved the green snake poem – typical of Habib to make so much out of so little. I can see it all over again through his eyes, the mesmerizing creature glittering as it was transformed with the changing light. And he was right – I had hardly thought it a suitable gift.

At about this time I was busy moving myself to another, smaller flat in West Hampstead because I couldn't afford to stay on in Mapesbury Road after the other girls had moved out. I also wanted something a little more private, with more space, fewer people and a kitchen to myself, if possible. I needed to earn, so took as many temporary typing jobs as I could, not wanting to be tied down to anything permanent that might get in the way of my music. There was singing to do in churches – very suitable and I loved it – but this tended to be unpaid.

Being wrenched apart from Habib yet again was very painful. I can remember that at this point I was beginning to feel disorientated once more and couldn't see what direction my life was supposed to take. I knew he would be coming back to London, but for how long? Was this just another interlude in both our lives, or something that could be built on?

By the time he returned to London from the States, I was well installed in my small flat, with my own kitchen and a big window looking out over a London back garden. Again, it was a very happy spell of some months – just comfortingly normal, with friends calling in, outings to the cinema, meals together with others, and me going out to earn spasmodically while Habib wrote at the desk that looked over the garden. He worked extraordinarily late hours, often writing well into the early morning, and then would get up later in the day, but he never seemed hurried. I loved waking up in the middle of the night to see the lamp still on and his bent head, accompanied by the very faintest sound as his hand moved back and forth across the page – a tableau of complete concentration. My brother Kev came around from time to time and revelled in the exchange of ideas and thoughts that flew around, galvanizing intense discussion and argument. He was looking very thin and vulnerable in those days, and needed to be fed. Many other friends turned up for meals, both English and Indian, as a result of which I rapidly expanded my culinary repertoire, learning how to make spicy food which few English people knew how to do in those days. We even splashed out on the odd bottle of wine for dinner, which was invariably called 'Blue Nun', appreciating it hugely as a rare treat. It all felt thoroughly right and utterly enduring.

I suppose I couldn't see the end of this existence because it seemed so natural a way to live. But then, hardly surprisingly, letters started to pile up from India. They were urgent, asking Habib to return immediately for he was badly needed. His theatre could not carry on without him, members of his family needed him, a niece's wedding was about to take place and he was expected to attend. At about that time, he developed a toothache and was determined to set up appointments with a dentist, which entailed treatment for many weeks. It was a good excuse to prolong his stay, for which I was very grateful.

Eventually his dental work came to an end, with a perfectly mended set of teeth to prove it.

The trip to the airport in a taxi, seeing Habib off to first stop in Germany en route to Delhi, was bleak. Neither of us knew how to make things feel any better, he trying to be light-hearted, talking about future theatre projects, while I was silent and weepy but not totally unprepared. For I knew full well that however difficult both of us might find it, he had to be in India in order to work. His travels around Europe had confirmed in his own mind that this was the case – that only there would he be able to be creatively true to himself. I respected this utterly but it meant that there seemed no way we could fit our two worlds together now. It was all too late, too star-crossed, strange and jarring to think all that had meant so much could simply disappear into the blue.

I remember well returning to the little flat on my own after that horrible airport trip, climbing slowly up the stairs to the first floor. Standing quite still in the doorway, I breathed in its emptiness and sense of desolation, feeling that its smallness was no longer cosy or familiar. There were some girls who lived in another flat at the same house, but they were not as interesting and warm-hearted as my Jewish friends of Mapesbury Road. In any case, they were about to move on, and I didn't want to chat with anyone, despite the loneliness. I actually felt quite ill and tired.

Berlin 15th Oct. 63

Jill darling,
I am seeing some lovely theatres here: 'The Rise of Arturo Ui', a famous play of Brecht, which I had not seen for

example – what a lovely production at the Berliner Ensemble. And tomorrow I shall see at the Ensemble 'The Threepenny Opera'. This evening is another theatre I am going to see 'Vasantseron', and an old German adaptation of 'The Little Clay Cart' by Feuschtwanger a contemporary of Brecht. I do not like this adaptation, but I am curious to see the production.

Have you heard of Charles Waverly, the American pilot, who dropped the Bomb on Hiroshima, and later began to suffer from hallucinations of guilt. It was a very good production – I mean the production of 'The Trial of Charles Waverly' in a theatre here in the east. Saw one more Brecht play at the Ensemble which I did not understand at all. But the most interesting experience was 'Schweik in the Second World War' at the Ensemble. I thought of you continuously during the performance. It was very good – a damn sight better effort than the Bernard Miles. Schweik was played as a straight simple character, yet wise. The décor was the same. Miles took it from Brecht, including the music box which gets lighted up during the songs.

I have written home asking them to postpone the marriage of my niece to December somehow; because now I just do not see myself arriving in time for it otherwise. I leave Berlin on 18th, Rome on 21st, Athens on 24th, Tel Aviv on 29th. Perhaps Tehran on 30th and Karachi on 4th of November.

Carl Harm's daughter wrote from Rome she would fix up an inexpensive hotel for me and would also take me round in her car. Splendid.

I stayed for 2 days in West and then moved. I am a guest here but I shall be back in West after the show tomorrow. Rosi came here for 2 days.

It was very nice to see her and talk to her, and know all about her present life. She is living with someone, which is good – but has many difficulties in her work. She had forgotten most of her English but it came back to her gradually as we talked on – and I was very glad indeed to meet her. So was she.

I have given a copy of my article about Edinburgh Drama Conference here in a theatre magazine and your address for payment for it in pounds some time in January perhaps.

This is a 'newsey' (sic) letter written under pressure of time. But news too had to be passed, hadn't it? More – later. But love, lots and lots of it. And look after yourself. And write. I am full of memories, haunting ones. All the wonderful food you cooked, things you typed, clothes you washed and pressed; and so much more. So much love. It was wonderful, night wahr? I felt foolish while saying goodbye and mused and mused for long later on.

How did you spend that evening? And now? What now? Kisses

Habib

(PS) 17 Oct. Thanks for forwarding the Swedish letter. They invited me for a week but so late that I cannot go to Stockholm now. But I got an invitation also from Switzerland for 5 days. So I am going to Zurich tomorrow

and shall be there up to 22nd – leaving Switzerland on 23rd for Rome. My Zurich address is Hotel Splugenscholoss, Splugenstrasse 2.

'And now? What now?' A question which preoccupied me greatly and to which I didn't have an answer myself. My spirits were not good at this time and I certainly didn't feel well. The memories and expressions of love grew all the more poignant as I thought of Habib going further and further away in the other direction, where another life awaited him. No amount of rational expectation had prepared me for this separation.

c/o madui 305 RIB colony Karachi
Tel Aviv 5th Nov. 63

Dearest Jill,
You were in time with your letter. But I do hope you did not send any letter to Athens. I got none.
It was sad Kev's behaviour. I do hope he gives up going to his psychiatrists and gets well which he naturally would – left to himself – I am sure.
But I am glad those girls left the house. Have you any plans about who you want to share the house with now? I can quite understand the emptiness there now. It even haunts me. It is better with Betsy. I am sure it is. But to add to the warmth, I send you again all my love and fondest thoughts and blessings.
What about Ehsan? Did you ever meet him again. He never replied to my letter but Aley did and asked for the poem of six metres. I have written a new one here yesterday,

which I had begun just before leaving Zurich. It is a good small poem but after getting the first 2 lines in a flash I had got stuck.

This was the type of poem about which I had no clear conception. So had to leave it to inspiration, and not force it. It was also possible it would get nowhere. But Ard Feder's house did it. Here it is in crude form.

> Sometimes I appear so ancient to myself
> That I want to deny my very past.
> Then I quit every City of Memory,
> Where my face is too familiar to the populace.
> I give myself a new name;
> With a new face I get attached.
> But even this new name begins to acquire
> Due to the effect of love, the same old meaning.
> I then want to get lost in the crowds;
> And stay friendless, nameless and low,
> Like a broken cup by the roadside;
> Or else, to prepare my soul for such action
> That every individual, every stone and every road
> Stares at me in amazement,
> And, even while recognising me, does not recognise me.

Athens was a lovely experience, though I am getting tireder and tireder from this journey – I walk so much. It is a beautiful city which you simply must visit some time. It is very inexpensive; the people are lovely and informal and warm, though I got cheated of £3 on the very first day. It reminded me of Spain a bit, but it has such a strong oriental *flavour about it, especially in its crowded markets. Well, that was the tip of Europe. And now I am on the tip of Asia, though Israel is like a European island in Asia. And tomorrow I shall be in the middle of Middle East; and the day after in Pakistan. I doubt if you have time to write to me in Pakistan, but I send the address, in case.*

Ard and Karah have hardly changed – neither physically nor otherwise.

But after many years since I saw them in Bristol, Marglid (?) is a young woman of 17 now, Amat a girl of 9 and Jan a boy of 12 and very dashing and handsome. A lovely bunch of children.

I went to Haifa and Jafa and now am with Shumoil and his wife Hamia and their daughter Anat (5) in Tel Aviv. Tomorrow I go to Jerusalem with them. Shumoil was with me in USA.

I rang up Maria in Athens. She is married. She was away from Greece, so she could not reply. But she was most sweet. We fixed up a time to meet but it clashed with a theatre appointment that got fixed for me later.

So we only talked on phone, though we were both very sorry. Maria asked most solicitously about you and mentioned that she knew all about me since your Munich meeting.

A nice English girl I met in Athens was Beryl Wood, 33A Clephare Rd, N. 1 (tel: Canonbury 5349). We went to the theatre together and dined. She is an architect. And I said she would like to meet Jill and Chliotu through Jill.

So why not ring her up, if you like. She must be back now,

Love Habib.

The sickness I had felt after Habib left had not started just then, on delivering him to the airport. It had been coming and going a couple of weeks before, even as I tried to ignore it. There were other signs as well, indicating that Habib might not have, after all, taken his entire self back to India. These were confirmed shortly after the letter arrived. It transpired that I was about six weeks pregnant – a huge and life-transforming prospect that was both frightening and joyous. It was certainly the most challenging condition I had encountered in my life so far. What brought me great comfort was that it was a natural outcome of love, though unexpected, and that developments would take their course, in their own good time. Of course, I wondered how my family would respond – and didn't look forward to finding out.

You ask if Habib knew about this before he left. He knew of the possibility, as I had mentioned my concern, but I guess he tried very hard not to dwell on it, there being little he could do at this stage. In any case, I didn't discuss it very much before his leaving and had no test, feeling it would be easier if I had a chance to think and to plan things on my own without pressure or panic.

I hardly made any attempt to find meaning in his poem. It wasn't the right moment to look into it deeply, and I remember finding it hard to understand Habib's frame of mind and myself feeling too impatient to try. Now, so many years later and with a clear mind, I find it very illuminating. In my understanding it reveals complicated feelings most subtly, suggesting an inner battle between a sense of his own destiny and the weight of responsibilities for past actions. It is almost as if he wants to shake off the accumulated karma of his own history and start afresh, but yet knows that he has a special duty to do something remarkable with his life. I feel he was only too aware that he would suffer the consequences of love and the responsibilities that attachment brings. There are also hints in the poem of the fame that was to come to him and the fear of that, together with a longing for ordinariness and the protection that anonymity offers.

Raipur, MP 21st Dec.'63

Dearest Jill
Yes, I know. You have every right to feel sore. It is 5 weeks since I arrived. Well, this is the first time I am writing any letter at all. But darling, not for a day have you ever been out of my mind. I was having the sweetest possible thoughts about you and your wonderful letter was so welcome. It came in very good time. And I began to visualise all kinds of lovely things about you. Actually this is the first time we have ever shared life at all properly and for any length of time – and the whole things haunts. I miss the warmth and the ease we shared over food, theatres and at home and the time spent with you amidst friends. My mind goes back to each detail whenever parallel situations occur striking a contrast and I even think of the peace with which we shared our monies. Oh thank you so much Jill darling for all that most wonderful period of time.
  Well, it is not an excuse I know – but I have been busy. Yes, from the day I arrived I started looking for work – and that struggle took up one solid month – every day of it almost, and of each day most of the wakeful moments.

In the end, all I got was Balwant's terrible play 'Ear of Corn' – in Urdu translation, to produce for the Punjab Govt., which it seems is likely to sponsor it for shows in the Punjab in the third week of February. So now I am busy first improving the darned text before I started rehearsing it from the 1st of January – the day I get back to Delhi. The play might be shown in Delhi around the second week of March.

But there is not a penny earned so far. I got down with 2 pounds in my pocket and have been living on it since. Lots of people and lots of groups were waiting for me to work with them, join them, produce plays for them it seems, but no money anywhere around. Got some terrible articles to translate, for which I would be paid Rs. 35/- or so – about £3 – some time in the future. The only two sources I expect some money from are 2 journals for which I wrote from London – one of them being the Illustrated Weekly of India of 8th December, carrying my article about Edinburgh. (Did you see it?) I went to Chandigarh in the meantime, along with Balwant, to arrange for the shows of his play there. Came here to Raipur on the 16th, though I have been trying to get here much earlier.

Jafri arrived from Lucknow the very next day after my arrival and stayed for about 10 tiresome days – tiresome because within 24 hours, Moneeka and I were having strained conversations and I didn't have the means for my own tobacco, leave aside hospitality. So one had to take a loan even coming here – and even the loan was not easy in coming.

Things are settling down now though – and there is much more peace at home. I am expecting lots of work actually but it takes time. In the meantime I am planning to write some more articles.

Next summer, the Education Ministry wants me to conduct a drama camp for the University lecturers like I ran 2 summers ago – and that is good. Then there are some lectures to come.

Regarding theatre work, India is much worse off now than a year ago.

And it would mean terrific hardship I think. But you never can tell. Things might suddenly improve.

I am using some of the old boys in my production, and Sushma (you don't know her do you?) who has had a baby on 2 December. Jogunder would be there of course – the fat comic boy – and Bashir, the large singer, is dying to join in too. But I cannot pay the cast just yet.

It took 5 solid days, if not a week, to do a thorough spring cleaning of the house – all my papers, letters of many years, manuscripts, books, odds and ends – all accumulated through the years, and further added to by the new piles brought from abroad. There being not enough space in the house, this was essential. And I feel better for it. I can plan more clearly now.

In the new year, I must get a book of poems published and if possible some plays. I have no idea when I shall be able to produce the 2 new plays I wrote before leaving India – but I hope some time soon.

I did not arrive here in time for my niece's marriage; but now the house is full of in-laws – a bother. Being home is nice though. My mother (about 80 or more) is happy – and it is so nice to share the humour of the house with my sister and her children.

Well, that is the whole story, Jill, of the return of the Prodigal Son – so far. But it is not all as bad as it might appear to you due to my writing from this great distance – coloured as it is, most probably, by the mood of the moment.

It was nice to meet Sham Bahadur again, who was in Delhi when I arrived – and stayed on for another 2 weeks. He inquired after you, as did Jafri and Jogunder.

I have composed no new poem in India, though I had an idea for one. But the idea must wait.

What else? Yes, Karachi was an interesting experience. I met an old friend of mine, Madui, an Urdu poet, nearly after 16 years – and that was nice – also a college fellow after 20 years – imagine. But the bugs and Pakistani filth in Madui's house kept me away all the 5 nights – and the terrible food gave me a touch of indigestion, which was to continue in India and get accentuated. It was only after reverting partially to semi-Western style of food that I regained my balance and saved some of the glow that a year abroad might have given me. I am fine now and feeling very fit.

It was warm, very warm in Delhi as also in Karachi – for a long time – in contrast – but recently I have been needing to wear my pull-overs. But the sun shines and it is lovely altogether – an envy for any Londoner.

To Ehsan too I could not reply in time. He might have left by now, though I am writing him now. Sinha too wrote that he is coming by March.

God help them all. I am glad though that they are coming. There would be more to share the motherland's boons – whatever they are.

I must get down to writing my report for New York – and some time in the future – if, if, if ... to write my own script of the Clay Cart for N.Y.

I am writing to William Gaskill of the National Theatre, London, too – and Kenneth Tynan, Martin Esslin, the BBC poet Macbeth, and John Calder of the Edinburgh Conference – in the vague hope that I can get to London again some time soon either for next year's Poets' Conference for the Clay Cart's production.

Altogether about 120 is the number of letters that I have to write to the U.S., Europe, Middle East and India – and most of this correspondence is related at best remotely to work – either here or abroad.

How are you spending your Xmas? In London with friends or at home? The thing for me to do was to greet you for Xmas with the neck-wear you had asked for – but darling I am afraid you have to wait for that. All my very best wishes are with you however for Xmas and a very very happy – a great New Year.

I am thrilled to hear you are doing fine. Do let me know how you are progressing with yourself, your exams, everything.

No, Ehsan lives too far out. Letters are easier to get at the address I sent you. I got the last one easily. I asked them if I could continue getting letters at their address. They have no objection. I would ask you to write to me on my own address, if you like. But for the time being, it might be better for all of us to keep the present arrangement, don't you think?

The letter was interrupted. I came back to it and read it again – it is a third grade letter – but I am not going to tear it and write another.

Who visits you nowadays? With whom do you spend your time most? And what sort of clothes do you wear these days? And what food do you eat? How often do you go to your doctor? Where do you work? – if not the same nice place you mentioned in your last letter. Do you get enough money? These and many more are the questions which keep cropping up in my mind perpetually.

It must sound a small world, my world, to you suddenly – I feel it has shrunk all of a sudden – yet I am terribly agitated about many things – like new themes for plays to write in order more quickly and thoroughly to become unpopular – the themes are such – I am furious (without any sense of humour about it) about the state of corruption, nepotism, bureaucracy, hypocrisy, flattery, and petty power politics in the country – and at the way people take it all so calmly. People of a revolutionary character, creating fearless literature and releasing more fearless action, are required to mind matters in a country like this country – but they are not anywhere around.

Instead you find Balwant Gargis, producing impotent literature, living a life without action – stupid.

But never mind. Here's love – lots and lots of it and many many kisses.

My greetings to all the friends. Have a good Xmas and lovely New Year.

Yours ever, Habib

I like this letter so much, Mukti, and I remember being overjoyed to get it – the longest Habib ever wrote to me, and full of warmth and interesting news.

By this time I was still living in London but had moved into the house of a friend of mine called Betsy Phillips, a rare and wonderful being. She was an art teacher who taught me when I was a child. I had loved her lessons and we had always kept in touch. It was she who offered me a room in her gloriously messy, art-filled home – I had not needed to ask her. After visiting me in the small flat I'd shared with Habib, she announced that it was far too lonely and that I should come and stay in her spare room. There was no question about it – I should not be living by myself. I greatly appreciated this unquestionably generous response. She was not censorious, either of myself or of Habib, nor particularly worried, which was most unusual under the circumstances! She seemed to be more than a little excited that a baby was coming along. I think the idea of a new life appealed very much to her sensitive, creative nature, and she knew I had loved Habib for many years, and that I would cope. That such a thoughtful person actually believed in me was very encouraging.

As it happened, this suggestion of my move into a house where there would be an eye kept on me amounted almost to a lifesaver. For in January of that year – 1964 – the winter was particularly wet and cold, and I contracted pleurisy. It started with a cold which developed into a great deal of pain around the ribs on taking in a breath. Walking was difficult and by the time I moved to Betsy's I could hardly get along at all. I had no doctor because until this point I had not needed one, so Betsy took me to hers who duly treated me and I recovered fairly fast.

Others did not react as Betsy had, to my news. Their responses varied from the horrified to the mystified, with quite a lot of anxiety thrown in. My mother was outraged about it and angry with Habib for his swift departure. She felt I had been abandoned. However, as soon as I assured her very firmly that none of this was helpful and that I was not unhappy to be pregnant, she calmed down and, with her usual warmth of heart, became practical and concerned. My father was too wrapped up in his own problems to take much interest in whatever might be happening to me, and I don't think my mother passed on my news to him for a good long time anyway.

The truth was that despite all the liberating effects of the hippie culture, free love and so on, being pregnant in the sixties without a husband was regarded as a very unfortunate state of affairs and at best an embarrassment to one's family. However, there was one very welcome and touching reaction – and it came of course from Granny, who was approaching her eighties at the time. She was actually the first person I turned to with my story. I went to stay with her for a night or two and felt I had to tell her what was happening, or else, knowing me so well, she would guess I was hiding something. She listened attentively, reclining on her chaise longue in her exquisitely chintzy sitting room, and then remarked, 'Well, my dear, babies such as the one you are expecting are known as "love children". In your case this is absolutely true. Now I think you should go off to bed early as you are looking tired.' And she gave me an especially warm hug and a kiss.

Living in the liberal atmosphere of Betsy's household was a delight but it was not to continue for many months. Her daughter Tabatha, with whom I had been at school, was due to come back home from a spell abroad and it was her room that I was occupying. Betsy insisted that space would be made for me and that she would like to house my baby too, but I thought it was too much to ask, as I already felt bad about having no money to pay for my accommodation. Then my sister suggested I go over to Ireland to stay with her, and Granny said she'd gladly pay for me to go to a reputed maternity clinic in Dublin for the birth. There was only one proviso Carley insisted upon – that I should tell no one I wasn't married. She asked me to say that my husband was busy producing a play in India, and as a result he could not come over to join me for the time being.

You will be shocked to hear this, Mukti, because your great-aunt Carley, of all people, would not think like that today. She is unconventional and one of the most open-minded of people I know, but fifty-odd years ago the concept of illegitimacy was quite different and such evasions were more or less the norm. I knew no one amongst the girls I had shared flats with or other friends who would have dreamed of having a baby out of wedlock and keeping it. I knew girls who had had abortions, and came across one or two who had produced a baby secretly and then had had it whipped away for adoption. In my case I was completely adamant that I wanted to raise my baby, and I was sure the difficulties lying ahead would not be insurmountable. Happily, this sureness never wavered.

At first I had hesitated to accept my sister's offer because I couldn't see how I would manage to tell the lies she needed me to agree to. After nine years of knowing and loving each other, a baby seemed an unsurprising outcome, requiring no shame or justification. Also – and this was a huge bonus – missing Habib was not so hard to endure under the circumstances, for there was a fullness of expectation where there would otherwise have been an emptiness.

The next letter came to my sister's house, just days before your mum was born.

New Delhi 15 April '64

My Dear Jill
I have just emerged from my production of Shakespeare's 'Taming of the Shrew' – and quite well. It is now being broadcast on 28th April, at 9.30 p.m (Indian Standard Time) – from Delhi – B ... in English of course, but I don't know what time it would be in Eire or whether you would be inclined to tune in.

I have been terribly busy. I got my theatre (NAYA THEATRE) registered – it even got a recurring annual grant of RS 1000/- from the Delhi Administration. This is very little but quite a help. I am now trying for a grant from the Ministry of Education for Brecht's 'Galileo' in Urdu for the World Science Congress in Chandigarh in September, and for a play by Shakespeare (in Urdu) for November. I have been re-reading Shakespeare profusely these days – loved 'Coriolanus' and 'Timon of Athens'.

Right now I am busy trying to do 'Raja Chambra aur Char Bhai' (King Chamba & the Four Brothers) the play I wrote 2 years ago. I am reading it to a group of friends and actors on 20th April and if I succeed in getting the subsidy I am trying to get for it from a mill-owner, I shall begin rehearsals from 7th May and put it up on 4 July.

I also talked about a Civic Theatre and the Municipality seems interested. But more important than that is the idea of a small professional bilingual repertory theatre (in English and Hindi), in which the Education Ministry seems interested. If this comes off, I have plans to prepare 2 or 3 Indian plays in English for foreign consumption and go abroad with the troupe. Yes, I am already thinking of and planning to go abroad again. One gets so sick so soon in India. A New York producer, a friend of mine, wrote to me that she thrice thought of calling me over, but each time, each play fell through and she could not get the money. But she says she wants me to direct one play for her some time. She would write to me as soon as she comes across the right play and money for it.

Sinha had to leave London suddenly because his father fell ill and died after his arrival. He wants to go back as also Ehsan, if they don't get anything worthwhile to do here much longer.

Met Lord Harwood of Edinburgh while he was here. He told me the Poets' Conference is off. Angadi, that bastard was here too. He appeared even more of a crook in Indian setting. I almost asked him for the shillings he fleeced you of.

I am sorry for these long gaps Jill, but I keep thinking of you. What a lovely place it sounds where you are. I wish I was there with you. Write to me how long you expect to stay there. A kiss, Habib

This was the last letter I was to receive from Habib for two years and it ends a significant part of our story. It is very difficult to conceive of something so abrupt, and I'm sorry that I can't make it a smoother telling. Shortly after I received it, your mum was born in Dublin. She was undoubtedly the most beautiful small creature I had ever seen, nothing less than a miracle of perfection, and her nature swiftly emerged as very cheerful. I know just about everyone thinks this of their first baby, at least about its beauty, if not its cheerfulness. But in addition mine, quite magically, had managed to acquire Indian feet – feet where the heels had a curve to them at the ankle and stood out more than usual – and these, together with a thatch of thick dark hair and huge inquiring eyes, made her doubly special.

 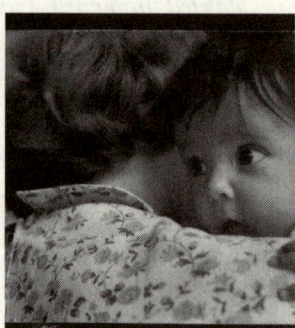

Jill with two-month-old Anna

I wrote to Habib and sent pictures, but received nothing in return. You ask me, Mukti, what I thought had happened. It occurred to me that he might have died, or at least become ill. I read and reread that last letter with its cool beginning, its preoccupation with theatre productions, and its wistful air at the end. At the time I simply didn't know, but felt that if no disaster had befallen him, he must have withdrawn. It was a horribly chilling sensation to feel that closeness simply disappearing as if it had never been, with no explanation.

Only much later did it occur to me that perhaps he absolutely didn't know what to do. Having a small person to care for who took up almost every waking moment meant that I did not sink into despair. Even so, his silence was insupportable – a dead weight on my life, and totally bewildering. Looking after my dark-haired daughter, who I so badly wanted him to see, made me wonder each day what momentous happening was stopping him from being in touch.

After two years of complete non-communication, I wrote to Habib to tell him the devastating news of my brother's death at the age of twenty-nine. Kev had been important to Habib, but I had no idea if he was still at the same address so I wasn't sure if the letter would ever reach him. I was surprised to get a reply. He wrote rather formally but comfortingly and asked after our daughter Anna, saying that he would love to see her one day. Inevitably, during those two years of silence, our relationship had changed.

At long last, he did manage to come to see us, and continued to visit from time to time, right up to the end of his life, as you know. There remained a genuine fondness between us and always unspoken efforts on his behalf to put things right. Undoubtedly, he did try over many years to pull together the different strands of his life. Despite the difficulties, I know that your remarkable grandfather got plenty of joy from seeing us all, including you three grandsons who were always kind and welcoming to him, even though you probably wondered what exactly his role was in your lives. On those brief and precious occasions we were a wonderfully united, contented family of three generations.

Top left: Jill and Habib, France 1996; Top right: Anna and Habib, France 1996; Bottom: Habib feeding his grandson Willoughby, France 2002

I will end this immensely long letter now, Mukti, with my warm thanks to you for your involvement. I'm grateful that you have been there listening and responding, for it made it much easier to recall Habib's letters and tell our story knowing that there was someone close by to receive it.

A Story for Mukti 203

PS: I have been rummaging amongst various papers, articles and letters of a later date. Habib sent this poem dated 25 June 1973 from the Balkan Hotel, Sofia, in Bulgaria, on the way to England to meet Anna for the first time. It's a strange one and haunting, but somehow apt.

> HOTEL BALKAN
>
> Sofia
> 25 June 73
>
> Jill, A poem, sort of :—
>
> I took a train
> To see the world
> And what I saw
> Was lovely
> As the train lurched forward
> The world moved back
> As the train ran faster
> The world slipped faster through my fingers
> Past all reckoning —
>
> The world was lovely
> But there was nothing more to see
> And I have not yet come
> To the journey's end —
>
> I thought you were with me in the train
> But I saw you in the woods
> I think I saw you
> In the glimmering light of the woods
> Amidst shadows of leaves
> Tree trunks dancing a polka
> All in a circle around you
> On a fast fast beat
> Your image dazzling white —
> Hair flowing
> It was a lovely apparition

When I read this today, I feel especially aware of my good fortune in having not only your mum, but you, Kim and Willoughby to love.

So much of Habib was lost to me, but through him, so much gained.

Epilogue

ANNA TANVIR

> Camp Raipur
> 19 ~~20~~th July 1990
>
> My dear Anna,
>
> I think of you constantly, ~~but~~ though I write so seldom. I would like to know how you are getting on. Kept hoping for quite some time now that I would perhaps be there sooner or later and then see you, but time passes and one keeps drifting, and never a chance in a long while to come to England. It is a long time since I saw you. A long time since Jill wrote to me last — a letter which sounded like she would like to write no more, as if she had written ~~the last~~ thing she wanted to. ~~was~~ It was a painful reminder of my filial failing — very justified, for which I have no proper reply, except to say that you must forgive me for my severity which comes over me occasionally, and it proves to be damaging both ways, for it haunts me too & fills me with a very sad memory. You are not an exception. Nageen has occasionally been its victim too. I am generally more understanding to the young who come to theatre, but once in a while I am off guard & let myself go in which I believe at that moment to be the truth — later realising that it is all relative, but by then I have done the damage & there is nothing else for it except ~~to~~ regrets as a forum that opens interval in which one holds oneself eternally guilty. I must be sounding rather old but no I am fine and active and busy and I think of you with love and of Jill with indulted and sympathy and tenderness. However all this is beginning to sound quite sentimental & I must stop ~~to~~ this drift. Do please let me have word as to how you are faring — your career at in life. And with about Jill. ... I hope to stage soon.

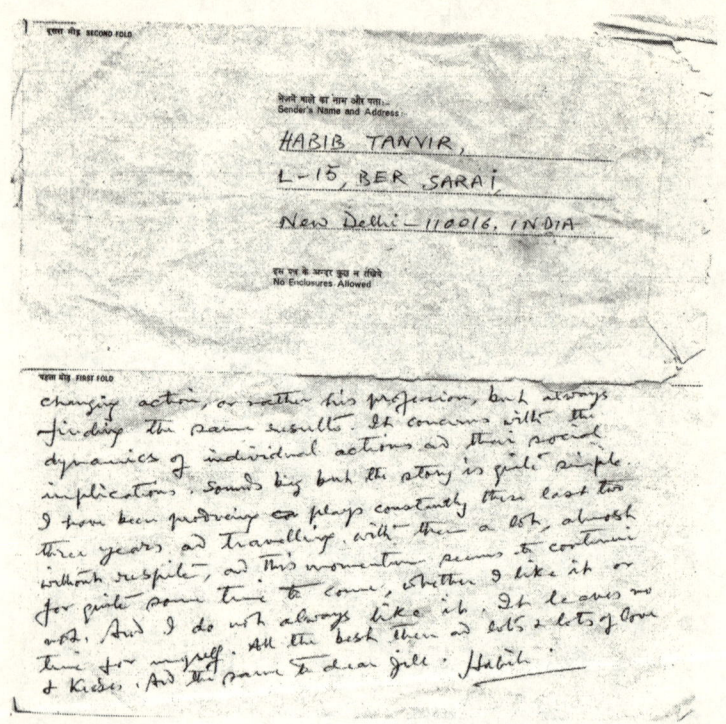

My first encounter with my father was unforgettable. It was not until I was nine years old that he came to meet me, by which time my mother had married, and I had a half-sister Vickie, who was as fair as I was dark. I had spent my childhood conjuring up his image in my imagination, inventing him over and over again, in more and more exotic colours. My mother had always talked of him, trying to give me a sense of my Indian heritage through her stories and descriptions. She would tell me that the movement of my hands reminded her of him and the way I put my head to one side when I laughed. She must have talked of him before I could speak, as I don't remember a moment of revelation. My father accompanied us in our daily lives in the imagination, and for me his image was so strong that he was somehow present despite his physical absence.

I was born in Dublin in a very smart nursing home, aptly named The Hatch. My mother had gone to stay with her sister Carley in County Carlow, but was in many ways very much on her own. I have never come across another woman who chose to take the boat across the Irish channel from England to Ireland to give birth to an illegitimate child during this period. The Catholic church had a hold on the Irish population and, backed up by the government, persecuted unmarried mothers and their children. They were hidden from society and children were separated from their mothers, and shamed parents disowned their daughters who were caught in this predicament. Luckily for my mother, her family was unconventional, not particularly religious and relatively unconcerned with respectability. The first person to come to the nursing home after I was born was an uncle, Peter, who had very dark skin and was assumed to be the baby's father by the Irish midwives. They were quite surprised when he, not being especially enthusiastic about babies, said he had only come to see the new mother. My mother didn't bother to enlighten the nursing staff; she pretended to be married, briefly calling herself Mrs Tanvir, in order to make a smoother path for the midwives and save other people much embarrassment. I don't think she herself minded about her marital status, believing entirely in her love for my father.

My mother moved house seven times during my first year. It was difficult for her to find a roof over her head at a time when unmarried mothers were so frowned upon. At last she settled with me in a beach hut in St Ives, Cornwall, used by swimmers during the summer to change out of their clothes into a swimming costume in private before emerging on to the beach. My mother and I were living there during the winter, and the sand would sweep in under the door. She had a small electric heater for warmth and sat typing other people's letters and essays to earn a modest living. Almost every day, she went out to ring her parents, waiting in a long queue to use the telephone in a traditional red box, with me in a pram beside her. Frequently, she met two sisters, who would also be waiting there. They'd chat away about their lives as dancers, and play with me while my mother talked on the telephone.

Eventually the sisters came back to the beach hut for a cup of tea. They were horrified when they saw the circumstances in which my mother was living; the wind was blowing very hard that day, and the sand mounted up from under the door. They persuaded her there and then to move out and share their house with them. They worked out a wonderful arrangement between them all: my mother did all the cooking and housekeeping for them in exchange for a roof over her head, while they danced for a living. Apparently, they all shared looking after me, and for a few months we were sheltered from the scrutiny of society's gaze. I learned forty years later that the older of the two sisters had given birth to a baby girl herself and had handed her over for adoption just a few months before meeting us. She was traumatized by her loss, and she told me much later that my presence and my mother's example were healing for her, but her story was a very common one at the time.

When I was growing up I knew of no other half-Indian children, so I was very aware of being different from everyone around me, including my family. The colour of my skin and hair attracted attention, especially when I spent time in Glasgow with my stepfather and younger half-sister Vickie, who had exceptionally blonde hair and big blue eyes. Vickie's father was a charismatic Scottish sailor (first encountered by my mother on her journey to India), who would take us both to visit his family who lived in a very poor area called Pollock where, as far as I know, there were no other Indians. I was frequently asked about my origins and felt very much on the outside of society. Strangely, this was not always an uncomfortable position to find myself in. The picture I had formed in my mind was that I had come from a great love between my adored mother and an incredibly exotic Indian poet who, for some mysterious reason, could never be with us. I pictured him swathed in clothes of gorgeous colours, wearing pointed Aladdin-style shoes – a source of constant entertainment with songs to sing and stories to tell. I thought of him as the explanation for anything in myself that stood out as different from those around me.

Anyone who knew my father at the time would recognize that my image of him was not far from the truth. I was nine years old when he arrived for our first meeting, clutching a chillum pipe that he puffed at continuously, clouding himself in wreaths of smoke, and wearing a large colourful shawl, a beret, a handmade kurta and stylish black jeans. My glamorous father was once described by a friend, writer Ben Faccini, as 'a mixture of Tagore and James Bond', and was every bit as exotic as I had imagined. He seemed to create magic wherever he went, and as for telling a good story, he recounted to me tales from the Mahabharata and the Ramayana hour after hour; I was mesmerized.

He came to Exeter where we lived happily with a large number of other people in a bohemian atmosphere. By this time, finding himself quite unable to adapt to the requirements of family life, my stepfather had taken himself back to the high seas as a ship's engineer and my mother found herself single, with two daughters. Earning her living as a singer proved complicated and she had to figure out a more practical career that would allow her to bring us up too. So she decided to change professions and set about getting qualifications as an English teacher.

My mother had left school at the age of fifteen and so didn't have the basic school exams she needed. Due to her mother's interest in Krishnamurti and dislike of institutions, she had attended a number of unusual schools where the focus was more on ethical living than acquiring school certificates. As a result, she was obliged to sit them in her mid-thirties, studying by correspondence so that she could stay at home with her young daughters. I remember how, with the pressure of approaching exams, she would become anxious about the books she was reading, and would shut herself up in her bedroom to type furiously for hours on end on her much-loved manual typewriter. Eventually she gained a place on a teacher-training course.

When I was six and my sister was four, my mother became a full-time student at Exeter University, which lasted for four years. To finance herself she took all sorts of part-time jobs in the holidays and rented out rooms to other students. We all ate together in a large kitchen, the centre of the household, eating vegetarian food off wooden plates. The atmosphere was friendly and informal, and our time was fairly unstructured, leaving plenty of room for singing and playing and reading and chatting.

A year after that first meeting with my father, he encouraged my mother to bring Vickie and me to India for a spell so we could get to know each other better. However, my father's work and family took up his time, so we did not manage to see him for longer than a few days. These we spent with him and his troupe while they rehearsed. Those brilliantly talented actors welcomed us into their lives and were particularly good with children, playing and singing with us, and Vickie and I were thrilled. My mother was waiting to join Rishi Valley School where she had been offered a teaching job; meanwhile, we lived in Defence Colony, New Delhi for four months. There, my sister and I played with a little boy who lived on the stairs outside the room we had rented. His grandfather was a dhobi who ironed clothes under a tree just beside our house, and they lived together at the bottom of the staircase. We had never met people like them before – an old man living with his young grandson, making do with so very little, and remaining, despite everything, good-tempered and friendly. We tried going to school and had pea-green uniforms (the colour of which made me feel slightly queasy) specially made for us, but we only lasted a week as we couldn't follow the lessons some of which were in Hindi. After that, we visited Mother Teresa's orphanage and helped look after babies and small children. This was heart-rending as some of them often asked us to take them back home, which obviously we weren't in a position to do. For both my sister and me, these experiences established a capacity to adapt and an enduring affection for India.

After this spell in Delhi, we set off on a three-day train journey to Rishi Valley, which we instantly loved for its beautiful environment and enlightened atmosphere. My mother taught English, and Vickie and I learned Telugu and yoga and listened to conversations with Krishnamurti. I had a small guitar, and the two of us would go to the dormitories and sing to the other children in the warm, soft evenings; and they would sing their own songs for us. This was my first experience of music being such a good way of communication across cultures.

Anna and Vickie at Rishi Valley School, 1975

My time in India when I was so young gave me a feel for my own heritage that has stayed with me. My mother's courage in taking my sister and me on such an adventurous journey allowed me to appreciate my father's work in a way I never could have otherwise.

At the age of sixteen, I decided to go alone from England to Delhi to stay with my father and his family for the first time. I arrived at the house one evening, having been picked up by my father from the airport in his old Ambassador, and I was introduced to his wife, Moneeka, and his other daughter, Nageen. We were all very polite to each other, and Nageen and I immediately sang together, but the atmosphere of the household remained tense, and it seemed easier for the village actors to absorb me into their homes, and in any case I loved being with them. After a few days, my father suggested that I go alone to meet some friends of his for dinner at the Taj Hotel. I arrived, inappropriately dressed in bright red dungarees and a saffron coloured shirt to meet a group of illustrious artists and academics who had no idea who I was as my father had somehow omitted to tell them. When the meal was nearly over, a great friend of his called Rajeev Sethi turned to me and asked me where I was from and why I was there. He was stunned by my response when I told him that Habib was my father and I was trying to get to know him. He had so many questions and wanted time to absorb my story so he invited me to join him for a tour of Rajasthan where he was researching for the Festival of India that was due to be held in London later in the year. I was taken on a magical journey, staying in palaces at night and visiting villages during the day, listening to music and meeting acrobats, puppeteers, magicians and dancers. Rajeev opened my eyes to the splendour, beauty and humanity of India, and I yearned to belong to such a fascinating country.

I returned to India when I finished my schooling, and lived there for a couple of years, working and living independently and learning as much as I could.

Then there was a very large gap of about twelve years when my father and I didn't meet at all, until one day, after I had been living in France for a couple of years, having acquired both a partner, Toby, and two small sons, my father telephoned. After a confusing conversation in which Toby thought it might be his own father pretending to be mine (Peter Sellers style), we gathered that he planned to come and visit the following day. I was amazed, and felt far from prepared for such a meeting. My mother, who lived nearby, was so surprised that she actually took to rolling herself a cigarette to calm her nerves, something she hadn't done for years. She kindly put on an old khadi kurta in the hope that this would make my father feel more at home. We were living in what was virtually a ruin – there were heaps of rubble everywhere and no proper plumbing or electricity and Toby's parents were arriving the same day! Looking back, I realize my father was probably the only one of us who felt at ease and coped well. He had a wonderful sense of humour which came to the fore when we all met in the garden. My father walked straight up to Toby and greeted him warmly, saying that he really should have brought a present for him from India. Reflecting briefly on this, he proceeded to remove his Indian pyjamas for Toby to put on. Toby's father was writhing on the grass with a painful tummy-ache, which was probably brought on by mounting tension as we all waited for this epic meeting of all four grandparents and the rest of the family. When I pointed out that undressing might shock Toby's parents, particularly his father who would have a spectacular view of his nakedness, my father replied, 'The sight of a pair of brown Indian buttocks will do him good!' The vision of Toby, clad in the proffered pyjamas that were at least eight inches too short, added to the bizarre comedy of the occasion.

I'm glad to report that he was to come many more times to France, mostly in this spontaneous and unexpected way, and we all got much better at being relaxed with each other. After the birth of my third son, my father tried to see us all as much as he could and we spent very happy times together. He taught his grandsons to eat with their hands and to put out candles with their bare fingers. He loved meeting my friends, particularly musicians and artists, and those who had made their own homes and who grew their own food. He was always willing to enter into discussion on any topic at any hour of the day or night, with an openness and light-heartedness most unusual for his age. His love of beauty, and his interest in other people and their creative projects never waned. It was touching to see him, in his later years a frail figure, taking the hand of Willoughby, the youngest, to visit the hens and ducks living at the end of our field. Nageen visited too, and I think she enjoyed meeting her nephews and singing and cooking with all of us in the big kitchen.

It's important for me that I have these memories and that they should still be so vivid. People seem to need to know their parents, and children who have been adopted often spend years searching for their real mother and father. As I didn't know my father when I was a child, I felt a great need to know him as I grew up. There were long spells when I forgot all about him. Then I would suddenly be reminded by a meeting with somebody who would describe him as having had a great influence on their life, or I would see him on a big screen at the cinema. Being the child of an absent father is one thing, but being the child of a famous absent father is doubly odd. I sometimes felt as though I was the *only* person in India who didn't know him. The difference in culture only added to the mystery – and to my curiosity.

Anna in Calcutta, aged 18

There were times when I felt I belonged to no one part of the world, and other times when I belonged to both the East and West. I certainly suffered from racist reactions when I was growing up, both in the UK and in India, but it was harder still to understand the response to illegitimacy. Nowadays it seems extraordinary that a child could be judged for being born outside of marriage. Even when I was small I found other people's feelings about this very hard to take seriously. Society and its ideas of social norms and conventions can result in cruel behaviour, and I hope that the publishing of my parents' story will help to open up the hearts of people to a greater understanding of the nature of love – a love that needs no legal structure to justify it, and does not die with distance and huge lapses of time between meetings.

I have often found myself in conversation with men and women of my own age who would describe my father as a 'father figure' for them, and it made me wonder about how

I too could love him in this way. I once asked him why he hadn't come to see my mother and me when I was very young. After an initial explanation about the pressures of Indian society and the difficulty of breaking with convention, which I found hard to accept given his reputation for radical and bold thinking, he went very quiet. After a very long time of reflection while he sucked at his pipe, he answered in a faltering voice that his own cowardice had prevented him from spending more time with us. This was a harsh but honest judgement and it opened the door for me to be able to love him. I loved him for his willingness to describe himself like this.

However, reading his letters to my mother has allowed me to understand far better what sorts of difficulties he faced, and to put myself in his place and know him better as a person, not as a famous dramatist. We had many conversations as two human beings trying to understand one another. I honestly believe this level of communication was a great relief to him – to be known as a real, vulnerable, emotional person who was aware of his own fragility, who had regrets and times of sadness experienced by all people who have a heart. He was aware of his parental failure towards me – 'filial failure' he called it in a letter he once wrote to me – and he knew that he had let my mother down during the years of silence after my birth. He was dogged by guilt, and he knew too that he had ultimately let everyone down by allowing himself to be so divided.

His memoirs convey a very different story of his relationship with both my mother and myself. Each of us chooses the story we tell of our own lives and the memories that form the landmarks along the line of our own personal narrative. His letters presented here with their consistent warmth and passionate need to be in touch entirely contradict the brief description of the relationship in the memoirs. I can only assume that over time, and driven by strong feelings of guilt, my father chose to filter out the thoughts and recollections that would distort the story he later found more comfortable to tell.

When a person is very well known for his work and his political thoughts, and has changed his country at some level through his endeavours, there is a real danger of turning him into some sort of deity, beyond the reach of ordinary human frailty. It's hard to imagine the bumpy road they have taken to get to that position of eminence. They become revered to such an extent that they are isolated from other people, and I know my father felt keenly the loneliness of being placed on a pedestal. It's easy to forget that these elevated beings have hearts, and therefore weaknesses, that as husbands and wives and parents, they are not perfect. It is hard to forgive our heroes and heroines for their human frailty, but I, as a daughter, have very much wanted to forgive.

A few years before my father's death, my mother and I went with my youngest son, Willoughby, to see him and his Naya Theatre performing in Germany. I remember hearing him say to the audience that day that his classic play *Agra Bazaar* had many themes, but above all it was about humanity and love, the most fundamental themes of all. He said it with such a grave expression, and in such a gentle tone of voice, that I knew he was telling himself too that these were indeed more important than any other themes – either in his plays or in his own life.

Habib and Anna, 1996

Habib at his grandson Kimani's first birthday party, France 1996

Family reunion in France, 2002

Acknowledgements

My heartfelt gratitude to all those who have provided me with unfailing encouragement, love and forbearance. Without them, this book could have become a lonely and quite overwhelming task to complete. My thanks, of course, to Anna, whose sustained interest and insightful contributions have been invaluable, and to my younger daughter Vickie and her family, always there for me, my sister Carley, my grandsons and my cousins Richard and Mireille Burton.

My thanks also go to Mita Kapur, my agent (of Siyahi, Jaipur) whose hard work and practical help made all the difference, and to my editors Ajitha G.S. and Bidisha Srivastava of HarperCollins India, a most diligent and patient pair. Thanks also to Rimli Borooah, whose generous comments were most welcome. I'm grateful for the friendly help given to me by Rani Ray and Partha Chatterjee, Phillip Hamoniaux, Marina Williamson, Astrid Sweetnam, Louise Belanger, Jim and Pauline Craig, Rachel and Kimwei McCarthy, who read through, or listened to, whatever was passed to them.

Many others have taken an interest in the writing of this book and offered useful comments. In particular I would like to thank Shakeel Hossain, Sarah Foster, Zarina and Anthony Kurtz, Florence Strauss, Zakiya Powell, Jalabala Vaidya, Sulabha Dixit, Mira Madhavan, Sangeeta Gundecha, Angela Hind, Janet de Vries and David Evans.

Finally, I would like to acknowledge the kind and very early involvement of Udayan Vajpeyi, close friend and companion of Habib, who first read his letters in 2009 (passed to Udayan by Anna) and believed in their value.